Taking the Devil to Court

Present Your Case

Taking the Devil to Court

Present Your Case

Marjorie Cole

Printed by
Companion Press
P.O. Box 310
Shippensburg, PA 17257-0310

ISBN 1-56043-225-X

For Worldwide Distribution
Printed in the U.S.A.

ACKNOWLEDGEMENTS

I want to thank the Holy Spirit for His constant and abiding help in guiding us in bringing together the truth of the Word of God to give us a better understanding and insight into the enemy's strategy.

I want to thank God for bringing helpers to walk alongside this project, see the need and roll up their sleeves to pitch in and help. I am especially grateful to Drew and Julie for their sweet spirits and expertise in preparing the manuscript for publishing and distribution.

Thank you to Maybelle and Sue for proofing and for Margie for typing the original draft.

Finally, I want to say "thank you" and "I love you" to my husband, Jarry, and for his prayers and words of encouragement and his great patience in allowing me to spend hours and hours at my computer. Of course, thank you to my beautiful daughters, Rachael, Sarah, Becky and Stephanie, who gave up their mom, day after day, to this book and the work it required.

Thank you God for your promise and direction in Habakkuk 2:2, to "Write the vision And make it plain on tablets, That he may run who reads it." Thank you, Jesus, that "The desire accomplished is sweet to the soul,..." Proverbs 13:19.

PREFACE

I have had the privilege of working in the field of counseling and psychology for over ten years. During that time my passion has been to help people be set free to walk in the joy and peace of the Abundant Life Jesus died to give us. I have never been particularly interested in the religious rhetoric and ritual that has been constructed around Divine truth, and have, in my own way, resisted it. I am not particularly interested in the political promises of two chickens in every pot or the pursuit of hyper-faithism, but have been deeply motivated to see the Kingdom of God come.

Over the years God, in His wisdom and patience, has allowed me to interact with some of His more troubled and broken sheep. I have had consistent exposure to the complex and deep seeded problems of people only to conclude what I already knew. The cliches and trite euphemisms we offer in place of the power and demonstration of God's Word have left us bleeding and dying on the battlefield.

The desire to make a difference, and my strong desire to know the truth, drove me to search out the mystery behind Satan's plot against the human race as I witnessed it in the destruction of their individual lives. Gradually the picture began to come together, a piece from here and a piece from there, like a giant 1000 piece puzzle. As the Holy Spirit would drop an idea into my heart He would show me the scriptural principles that supported it. As I applied these truths to individual situations, people started experiencing freedom. Eventually the diagram of Satan's strategy came together and was complete enough to form a functioning whole. The explanations and understandings were in agreement with the Scriptures and the outcomes were in agreement with what would be predicted or expected. (This is the ideal we look for in any scientific method of experimentation, where results are significantly correlated with the identified cause enough to be able to predict future outcomes.) The nice thing about this was that though I did not claim to be a theologian, nor do I read Greek or Hebrew, I was thrilled with the common sense logic these explanations were making.

Keeping the truth simple does not make it any less profound or powerful nor does it require super-spirituality as a pre-requisite to freedom. I have tried to put these concepts into a language that is understandable and accessible to the general population of the afflicted. Some of the material you may find difficult to accept because of the allegories and analogies used to explain them. Others you may find to be contrary to some of the theology you have come to rely on. I am not here to argue with you or talk you into something. I am writing this to tell you what I have found and what seems to be working, and invite you to look past the parables to find the spiritual truths hidden there in.

Many who have pioneered in the fields of inner healing and deliverance have worked faithfully to lay the foundation for some of the significant breakthroughs we have seen in the last ten years. We are continuing to learn as God gives us His revelation into the mysterious inner workings of the spiritual world. Some are beginning to use those keys to unlock the prison cells of those who have been held captive by the devil all their lives, prisoners in their own souls. I do not wish to make these truths a matter of controversy or division. There is enough of that in the Body of Christ. I ask you to simply allow me to share with you what I have discovered and think it through for yourself. If what I have found is true, you too can see people being set free from mental anguish, fear, depression, sexual perversion, pornography, heartaches, headaches, backaches, paralysis, financial bondages, broken and dysfunctional relationships, and demonic oppression of every kind.

God's truth is here to heal us. He is the Wonderful Counselor. He is the faithful Witness. He is the One who does the work of inner healing and deliverance. We are not the counselors. We are aids to the Wonderful Counselor. We simply facilitate His working of life recovery in those who seek His help.

We ask you to read this book with an open mind, and ask God for His Spirit to bear witness to your own soul, as to the truth of the words written here. We are all weary with fads in the Body of Christ and using the Gospel to further our own ends. We are all tired of living, frozen in the mediocrity of our traditions or hanging off the outer edges of extremism. We have seen truth isolated in pockets of effective evangelism here and there, but it is time to walk in balance and allow the Word of God to be integrated into our whole life. We have a mind, emotions, a will, a body, and a spirit. We have financial and physical circumstances in which we live in. We carry a mandate from Heaven, a destiny, mission and purpose. Some of us have children. All of us have a new inheritance in Christ. All of these things are important to Jesus Christ and He is the answer to every need in any area of our life. He is mindful and merciful and loves us very much, with the kind of love that bids us come and follow Him, trust Him and let Him intervene in our lives. His Abundant Life is for all of us. He wants us to recover that life.

AN IMPORTANT NOTE:

Deliverance and inner healing are a form of art much like script writing or painting. There are basic structures and principles that can be taught, as well as learned, by the student, but the fabric and essence of the story or the picture belong with the author or artist. I can tell you something about how to paint a picture or tell a story. I can identify some generally accepted information like painting the background before the foreground, or placing the hero in his or her ordinary world in the opening, but I cannot tell your story or paint your picture.

The same is true of inner healing and life recovery. The journey is yours; the choices, the assets and liabilities are yours to manage or dispose of, as you will. As with health care, there are accepted standards of care and practice; and even as each physician applies those standards with varying degrees of success, the final outcome in the journey belongs to the patient.

As care givers, however, we undertake great responsibility in assisting others in their healing, and understand that much of that healing still lies within our expertise and skill as helpers. I urge you, therefore, healers of the breach, to allow the Great Physician to heal you before you work with others in their journey to recovery.

We commit to you our deep interest in your healing, but remind you that this book is not intended to be a substitute for your own seeking out of God's will, and, if you choose them, the recommendations of your physicians and health care professionals. We are simply here to offer information to help the reader become more aware of the things we have found helpful in our mutual quest for increased well-being and abundant life.

The publisher and the author of "Taking the Devil to Court," are not responsible for the outcome of any techniques and/or services offered or referred to in this book, and expressly disclaim all liabilities in connection with the fulfillment of expectations held by the reader in regard to information or testimonies contained therein. The author and publisher also are not responsible for any damage, loss, or expense to person or property arising out of or relating to the practices of, or understood applications of, any of the procedures or techniques discussed in the book, "Taking The Devil to Court".

ONE FINAL NOTE:

Though the examples and stories told in this book are true, details that would identify specific people have been changed to protect the personal privacy of the individual.

CONTENTS

TAKING THE DEVIL TO COURT

INTRODUCTION

TAKING THE DEVIL TO COURT

Before we can take the devil to court, we need to have a clear understanding of who we are as believers and the crimes he's committed against us. Our identity includes the right and responsibility to exercise the free will God has given us to make choices. Much of what happens to us is determined by what we believe. What we believe determines our choices. Our choices determine what happens to us, and the cycle continues.

Truth is the great liberator that breaks the cycle of bondage and defeat. Both God and the devil influence our thoughts, but the final choice by which we must live is the one we make! The devil invades our lives through the openings created by the sins of the generations. His war efforts against our souls are always spearheaded with lies. He intends to wrestle away from us our freedoms and intimidates us with fear. He assaults us and works to fragment and divide our minds. He weakens our wills and wraps his lies around us, creating an environment for destruction called strongholds.

Our first and only system of defense, and our strongest protection against the liar and his bondage is the truth. The truth of God's Word provides the protection and the platform for resisting the devil and taking back what he has stolen from us. The enemy wants me to think I have no choice and that I am hopelessly strapped into a life of loss and futility, held captive, a prisoner in my own soul. God wants me to be free.

Many of us are struggling just to survive. We are hesitant and fearful, more often the victim then the victor. Jesus said, "I am come that they might have life, and life more abundantly," John 10:10. God wants us to understand that we are more than conquerors. He has given us His grace and good cheer, and encourages us to live in the freedom His truth has provided through the victory of the Cross.

THE SPIRIT OF THE LORD IS UPON ME

Isaiah prophesying of the Christ in Isaiah 61:1-4 said "The Spirit of the Lord God is upon Me, Because the Lord has anointed Me...to heal the brokenhearted, to proclaim liberty to the captives, and the opening of the prison to those who are bound,..." Jesus proclaimed this to be the purpose of His coming to us and initiated His public ministry on earth with the reading of this passage from Isaiah (see Luke 4:18).

The captives, the bound, the brokenhearted, the oppressed, the downcast...where are they? If we would live in the forest, they are the trees. Do we see them, or have they become so familiar that we no longer notice them? Are they not all around us, everywhere? Was He talking about a prison house liberation, down at the local county jail? Was He speaking about open heart surgery? If we can interpret these words on an internal level, it is not difficult to understand His reference is to the condition of our souls.

Jesus made it clear that the kingdom which He came to possess, the one of which He spoke was "within" (Luke 17: 20-21). The contest between God and Satan is for the kingdom that is held in the hearts and affections of people. The battles between God and His adversary are for the souls of men, fought within the very hearts of those men.

Isaiah describes those hearts more graphically in Isaiah 42:22. "But this is a people robbed and plundered; All of them are snared in holes, and they are hidden in prison houses; They are for prey, and no one delivers; For plunder, and no one says, 'Restore!'."

Who will deliver, who will cry for their restoration? He answers part of that question in Isaiah 61: 4. The Spirit of the Lord God that was upon Christ will raise up "trees of righteousness" who will, in turn, "rebuild the old ruins, they shall raise up the former desolations, and they shall repair the ruined cities, the desolations of many generations. The "ruined" city needing to be "rebuilt", the "old ruins" the "desolations of many generations" that God wants to raise up can as legitimately refer to the human life as they could be to the war-torn towns of Israel.

THE POWER OF THE GOSPEL

The power and truth of the scripture to defeat our enemy are never more real and convincing then in its power to change lives. The Gospel's power to heal crosses generational lines, socio-economic systems and cultural barriers. It transcends time and anticipates change. The Word is never old or out dated. If anything is obsolete or out of touch, it is us. Our denominations and religious groupings may be slow in recognizing the paradigm shifts society makes, but the Word of God was there before the trend appeared and will be true long after it is gone. The Word speaks truth to the simplest and the most complex of human needs. The truth needs no defense because it will take care of itself. God's truth is all the power we need to defeat the demons of Hell, wherever we find them and to take back what they've stolen from us. Though it may pose a challenge to our theology, the Word of God is not daunted by what it sees. There is nothing known to or experienced by humankind, be it tragedy, emotional fracturing, or demonic infestation of the human life that is a mystery to the Omniscient, Almighty God. He has already addressed every human need, every case scenario, and every situation possible to experience on the basis of His Word, the Truth. We must do the same if we are to get God's results.

SCRIPTURAL FOUNDATIONS

Scriptural principles form the footing and foundation of legal rights and spiritual authority of the believer. They also present the first critical element in inner healing and deliverance. Before we can defeat the strongman entrenched in the ruined city-soul of our lives, is to understand what it is that has given him legal right to be there in the first place.

The concepts and procedures highlighted in the following pages are drawn from God's Word. They provide the scriptural basis for the strategies for freedom and warfare that seem to be part of the progressive revelation of truth that the Holy Spirit has referred to in Colossians 2:1-3. He wants our hearts to be encouraged, "being knit together in love, and attaining to all riches of the full assurance of understanding, to the knowledge of the mystery of God, both of the Father and of Christ, in whom are hidden all the treasures of wisdom and knowledge."

Many have prayed and labored in the areas of inner healing, deliverance, and counseling. Their work and observations are transdenominational and include a compilation of efforts ranging from theology to psychology. Though techniques used in deliverance and inner healing display a broad continuum of belief and practice, those that are legitimate are founded on the principles of truth as based in the Word of God. This work is not an exhaustive but exemplary documentation of the profound and powerful work being done by the Holy Spirit in the area of healing and deliverance.

I have worked many years in the field of counseling-psychology, and refer the reader to the work of others who have given themselves unselfishly to the Lord in pioneering the works of inner healing and restoration. Freedom and healing in both emotional and physical areas are the manifested fruit of applying the scriptural principles of deliverance, spiritual warfare, authority, and inner healing to the strongholds and wounded lives of those ravaged by the Liar.

CHAPTER ONE

PRESENT YOUR CASE; ISAIAH 41:21

STRUGGLING SAINTS

Jenny was convinced that she was never going to change. "I don't know what good this will do. Everything I have ever loved gets taken away from me. How can I believe God is good when He lets all this bad stuff happen to me? If I do love Him it is only in my head. I really don't believe He loves me...I just don't know how to get there."

Sara was depressed, trying to pull herself back together after a third emotionally abusive relationship with a boyfriend. "I don't know why I pick all these needy guys. Nobody liked me in school. They all made fun of me; I was too tall, and always felt like there was something wrong with me. I just wanted to help."

Ted was confused. His wife had left him and became pregnant by another man. He was torn between letting her go and loving her through this dark valley. "If I get involved and let my feelings go, I'll get hurt again. If I don't make a commitment to anything, I won't get hurt."

Matt was perplexed. "I have to live with the pain. They will think bad of me if I tell them what I really think. Why should I commit to anything, I'm just going to mess it up anyway. I don't want to hurt anybody. They need for me to be strong."

Mary was done trying. "What's the use of serving God? Every time I try to live for Him, I get attacked, things go wrong. It's just not worth it."

Maybe you have never had thoughts or said things like that to yourself. If so, you probably do not need to read this book. If you are still curious, however, perhaps the next 60 seconds and these three questions can help you decide.

1. Have you ever felt like Jenny, Sara, Ted, Matt, or Mary?
2. Are you struggling with problems that just do not seem to go away, no matter how much you try to work through them?
3. Do you feel stuck? Going backwards? Does it seem that the harder you try to serve Christ the worse it gets?

If you answered "yes" to any of these statements, welcome to the war! Please continue reading for further instructions.

All of these situations have several things in common. Analyzing them from a non-technical point of view reveals that conclusions about how we view things are drawn from our experiences. We commonly embrace our perceptions as truth, in spite of the fact that the assumption is not always valid.

Lies form the foundation of Satan's operation in us. He uses our beliefs to lay the ground work for the destruction he desired to bring into our lives. Through lies, the enemy creates the strongholds and systems of pain and bondage that hold us in captivity. Each of us finds our own way to cope. We often choose to live in denial, compensating for living our lives based upon lies by believing more lies. If our lives in Christ are unhappy, unfruitful and defeated, can we say we are living in the truth? The truth as Jesus describes it says, "I have come that they might have life and life more abundantly," John 10:10. I am not here to proclaim a life of ease and extravagance for the believer, or to deny the place of suffering with Christ or that being persecuted for righteousness sake has no place in the believer's experience. What I am saying, is that to live short of the peace and joy and assurance Jesus promised us, is to live in less then His fullness.

The time is short and the need is urgent. Many of us professing faith in the shed blood of Jesus Christ are still imprisoned within the confines of our own lives, still struggling with "thy Kingdom come, thy will be done" in us. We are bound in patterns of destruction, frustrated with ourselves and unsure about God. We cannot free others when we are helplessly stuck ourselves. We wrestle with our own personal feelings of condemnation and abandonment while leaving the work of God's Kingdom is left undone. The lost stumble on in darkness, the weak keep dying. We are like prisoners of war being held captive in our own souls, not unlike the condition of those Isaiah described in chapters 42 and 61. We are a people robbed and plundered; snared in holes, hidden in prison houses; for prey, and no one delivers; For plunder and no one says, "Restore!."

Jesus wants to set His people free. "I have held My peace a long time, I have been still and restrained Myself. Now I will...bring the blind by a way they did not know; I will lead them in paths they have not known. I will make darkness light before them and crooked places straight. These things I will do for them, and not forsake them." Isaiah 42:14-16, The LORD is coming as the Righteous Son, as, "... a light to the Gentiles, to open blind eyes, and to bring out prisoners from the prison, Those who sit in darkness from the prison house." Isaiah 42:6-7.

Jesus said, "If you continue in my word you are my disciples, indeed and you shall know the truth, and the truth shall set you free," John 8:32. The power of these incredible words is becoming reality. God is giving us the end times strategy and showing us how to use the weapons of truth. He wants us to use them to set the captives free. He is showing us how to apply His truth to the human heart in ways that are practical, intentional and specific. He is teaching us to apply the eternal truths of scripture to our temporal and immediate condition in a way that begins to release people into a new fullness of faith and freedom before our very eyes.

8

THE PERPLEXING PROBLEMS

Troy was desperate. " There must be something more. If it all depended on me and my choices, it would have been done by now. If it is my sin that's hindering me, and I've repented, shouldn't I be free? I can't live another 15 years like this."

Too many people's lives reflect this dilemma. Our first response might be to group them into a stereotypical category of backsliders. We might even be tempted to just leave it at that. God's married to the backslider, Jeremiah 3:14. It's His problem. But, just what does go wrong with people, many of whom who start out with God, some even in great enthusiasm, who several weeks or years later, have fallen away? What about the ones who only go so far and then get stuck and don't seem to grow? What about the ones who get clobbered every time they try to make a move toward God? Things keep going wrong in their life until they conclude that stepping out for God only brings trouble.

Alicia had accepted Jesus Christ as her personal Savior as a child, and had rededicated her life to Him 15 months ago during another one of her frequent hospitalizations. She spoke openly of her faith in Jesus Christ as her Savior, and even brought her Bible along to treatment, for which she usually received no small amount of persecution. She felt hopeless, a "smoldering flax", entrapped in a social, psychological system that had limited answers, and disappointed by the church, who questioned the authenticity of her salvation. Instinctively, she knew Jesus was the one thing she had left, and even though all the perplexing circumstances remained, she knew He was her only hope.

Constance had been a Christian for 15 years, and had even attended a local Bible college for a year. She was born to a mother who beat her and practiced witchcraft. Recently she began to experience nightmares and mental images that were too hideous to share with her believer friends, afraid they would think she was crazy. She lived in chaos and denial, and had a hard time reconciling the events of her life with the things she wanted to believe. Why, if she were normal, did she feel an overwhelming rage when she tried to worship God? She was torn. She wanted to serve God, but felt an over powering disgust rise up inside her each time she walked into the house of God. She heard voices inside her head that mocked the things of God, calling His people and His Word, garbage. She knew these things were more then just normal, run of the mill temptations that were common to the believer. How could it be right to feel rage toward two of the dearest, sweetest prayer warriors of the church when they came to pray with her at the altar? All she could think of was hitting them.

"If this is me and the things I'm feeling and hearing are me, then, there is no hope for me," she cried. "If this is the freedom Jesus has come to give me, how is it different from the bondage I experienced before I knew Him?" She had periods when she could pray, but they didn't last that long. An uncanny and constant plague of "bad luck" seemed to follow her like a relentless swarm of locusts, eating up even her smallest victories. Denial, lying and despair sabotaged anything good that tried to come into her life. What was the power that kept her in bondage? Was it fear of rejection that caused her to tell people what they wanted to hear, or was it distrust and the overwhelming need to control that prompted her to keep back information from others to secure and maintain her advantage over them?

ARE THEY SAVED?

Do the stories described above represent extreme cases that can be easily reasoned away with theological catch-all explanations and generalizations? "They aren't really saved." "They're not willing." "They're under stress." "They are mentally ill and need to stay on their medication." "They are demon possessed." "They were not sincere." How many of these people have come to the church for help only to be labeled by our judgments and referred out to the world for help. Do any of these responses bring hope or testify to the power of God's truth? Many opinions but no solutions have already been tried and applied to no avail. The frustration and failure levels remain high and go unchallenged. Is there an answer or are some people just unsavable? Are some doomed to destruction in spite of their desires to be saved? What would Jesus have us do? Did He chide the woman who had the infirmity for 18 years for her unconfessed sin, or her unbelief, or did He just know what was wrong and do what needed to be done? "Think of it", He said as He pondered her condition in front of His critics. "So ought not this woman, being a daughter of Abraham, whom Satan has bound – think of it—for eighteen years, be loosed from this bond on the Sabbath?" Luke 13:16. He did not expect the religious experts to understand and was not caught off guard when they did, in fact, miss the point. Fortunately, He did not need their approval to accomplish the will of His Father. He was secure enough in His Father's love to know He did not need the recommendations and approval of men to be somebody. He was able to go against His enemy with fearless authority and call upon His Father's utmost confidence, as can be seen in His perfect record of miracles. Jesus knew how to help people and is still the perfect solution to every human need, whether we ascribe to Him or not, whether we describe the need for healing, or deliverance or salvation.

If these are extreme cases, we relegate to padded rooms and anti-psychotic drugs, then what about the worship leader, who broke out into uncontrollable laughter, mocking the holy things of God when confronted in the pastor's office by his counselor? Or what explains the sweet middle aged believer who gave himself unselfishly to foster care parenting, and church work, who broke out into convulsive shaking and uncontrollable contortions on the church floor after coming up for prayer for physical healing? What about his mysterious medical problems that seem to evade diagnosing by the best that medical technology had to offer?

The physical symptoms and spiritual conditions range from common to bizarre, but the stories are true stories of genuine believers. Many of these people, like the woman bound by Satan for 18 years, had already exhausted the medical and secular resources looking for help. Some had been in the church for years. What will we do? Cliches will not suffice and our theological explanations fall short in accounting for much of what they are experiencing. To refer them to the "professional counselors" and reassure ourselves that we have done our duty is deceptive and unbiblical. Proverbs 24: 11-12 leaves us without excuse. "Deliver those who are drawn toward death,… If you say, 'surely we did not know this,' does not He who weighs the hearts consider it? And will He not render to each man according to his deeds?" Many passages in scripture instruct us on how to care for our own, but none instruct us to send the wounded into the world for counsel. If we do not know what to do, it is not because He has not given us the answers.

GOD IN A BOX

Could the church be missing the answers to these problems because we've put God in a box? Do we restrict His working to fit within the guidelines of our definitions of healing, deliverance, and demonic activity? We may have to reread the Word of God for what it says, and not for what we think it says if these people are going to get the help they so desperately need. We need to reexamine our Lord's command to heal the sick, cast out devils, and raise the dead. Has the modern church come to believe it has outgrown the need for deliverance, thinking of demonic activity as primitive and barbaric? Are we afraid that acknowledging the presence of the demonic will empower it? Do we exempt ourselves from the notion of Christians having demons because we find it fearful to think a believer could be simultaneously, both a Christian and in need of deliverance from a demon? Does that possibility contradict the Word of God, or our interpretation of it?

Both the correct interpretation of the scriptural position, and the need for a correct understanding of the personal experience, are essential to the successful resolution of these problems. Correct diagnosis is imperative if these people are going to get the help they need. To suggest a believer is in need of deliverance undermines nothing of the grace of God or the power of salvation in their life. It actually lends itself well to the work and definition of sanctification, the ongoing work of restoration and establishment of the presence of the Holy Spirit with in our lives. To suggest, for example, that a person look back to his or her generations to discover patterns of dysfunction, takes nothing away from our need to obey God and take personal responsibility for our sin. As a matter of fact, the Life Recovery approach to inner healing and deliverance makes personal choice the pivotal piece connecting God's truth and our present circumstances with future outcomes.

THEOLOGICAL JARGON

Getting help for these people means getting past the theological jargon and futile discussions about Christians being exempt from demon occupation. We would do well to take a look at the situation with our eyes open. What is the difference if demonic activity manifests in our life, on the inside, by demonstrating its presence and influence in panic attacks, chain smoking, a cancerous tumor or hearing voices; or on the outside, by accidents, persecution or misfortune? Why do we distinguish between physical and psychological needs when Jesus is the answer to both? He is our Healer and our Deliverer. The Word uses both deliverance and healing interchangeably to describe His work among the multitudes. We cannot split the human life into compartments. We are made up of body, soul and spirit. They are created to function together and together they create an environment for life. Each is essential to function of the whole. The soul is made up of the mind, will and emotions. The mind is housed, for all practical purposes, in the brain and functions in the processing of thoughts and ideas. The emotions are described as feelings and are often attributed to an area called the heart. The will is the guardian, the gate keeper and the covenant maker that considers options and information and devises a plan of action or an opinion. Death is the condition in which the body, soul and the spirit are separated from one another. The enemy's work is to fragment us and bring us into premature death.

The nice neat little pat answers like, "Just give it to Jesus, or Just trust God," will not cut it any more. For many, those words only serve Satan's purposes to condemn them and to drive them deeper into their hopelessness and despair because, "they've already tried that." Who am I to question if these people were never saved in the first place? Many of them confess Jesus Christ came in the flesh, died on the cross, and rose from the dead three days later, the same way that I do. One woman who was struggling with a spirit of rage and hatred, when asked if she was saved said, " I know I am saved because I know who Jesus is and what He did for me. Without Him I am nothing."

Frustrating people by asking them to doubt their salvation is not an effective way to help them stand their ground with confidence or take their authority as believers to fight the devil. There may be a few who are truly deceived about their salvation, but we are probably in greater danger of condemning the innocent then in pardoning the guilty. Jesus said, "a tree is known by its fruit," Matthew 12:33. Seeing apples on trees is the most common way to discern it to be an apple tree. But how do we know it from any other tree in the dead of winter if not by its shape, its history, and other physical distinctions? The only fruit some Christians have produced is the desire to produce fruit. God does not call us to judge anyone's salvation. If Jesus is not ready to quench a smoldering wick or crush a broken reed, can we do anything different? We would do well to discern the motives and intents of their hearts and be busy about our Father's business rather than judge their salvation. We would do better to understand the enemy's strategies for destruction and leave the judgment of their salvation with the Lord.

POSSESSION, OWNERSHIP VS. OCCUPATION

To believe that a Christian might have a demon is NOT the same as to be demon possessed. Demon possession in the English use of the language implies ownership, or occupation to the point of complete control. Webster defines the phrase, "to possess" to mean to have as property; to own, or to enter into and control firmly. The word possession can mean ownership, or control and occupation of property. Ownership, occupation and control, however, do not mean the same thing, nor can those words always be used interchangeably. I can function as a landlord, owning a house I do not occupy or I can function as a renter, occupying a house I do not own. The confusion surrounding the word "possession" has left the church in the western culture in a restrictive and difficult position.

Ownership means legal measures have been taken to give title or proprietorship to the individual possessing the documentation to verify that an object, or piece of

15

property belongs to them. Occupation means to fill up as in space or time, to take or have control of, or to reside in as owner or tenant. It can also mean taking control of an area, or property as when a foreign military force occupies another country, not unlike the illegal occupation the enemy tries to establish in our lives in his war efforts against us.

Understanding the two different definitions of "possession" helps us clarify the issues of demonic occupation. It is not logical to say that someone can be owned by two contrary forces at the same time. It is obvious that a person cannot be owned by God and the devil at the same time. One is either going to heaven or going to hell. Salvation is not a percentage deal. Just as a baby is either born or it has not yet been born, we are either saved, born into the family of God or we have not yet been born into the family of God. Salvation settles the question of ownership. On the other hand, it doesn't matter how nice people may be, according to the definition of possession as ownership, if they are not saved they are possessed by the devil because they are owned by the evil one. The extent to which he may control or occupy them will vary with the individual, but the question of ownership is clear. They are his property because they have not been translated into the Kingdom of God's dear son, (Colossians 1;13).

So the first question becomes, who owns you? Who possesses the title deed to your life? If you are saved, the Lord holds the deed to your life. He owns the house, regardless of what kind of shape it is in or if rats live in the basement.

RATS, GARBAGE AND THE KING

When we get saved, the King buys the house. But, just because the King owns the house does not mean the rats living in the cellar leave. The King may own a palace

16

that is occupied by rats. The rats, however, do not own the castle in spite of the fact that they do occupy parts of it, probably to the king's dismay. Because he is the owner, he has the right to overpower the imposters and exterminate those whom he so chooses. If rats can inhabit parts of the king's house, couldn't demons occupy parts of the as yet unregenerated, unsanctified temple of the Holy Spirit found in a believer?

Salvation and sanctification are not the same thing. Salvation, like birth, happens in a specific moment in time. Sanctification is a process of restoring, rebuilding and refurbishing the house to the King's specifications. Sanctification is the work of the Holy Spirit that extends over the life-time of the believer, to develop and mature the life brought forth in the new birth. Just as salvation and sanctification cannot be used interchangeably, neither can ownership and occupation, or possession and demonization be substituted one for another.

If possession means ownership or occupation, demonization describes the continuum or range of demonic activity in a believer. The term demonization can refer to the ground still held, occupied, or controlled by the evil one. It is used to describe the strongholds, those areas not yet yielded to the will of God in the life of a believer. Believers can be demonized to any point along a continuum that stretches from momentary faltering of faith to persistent sin. Let it be known that, as Paul cautioned us in Romans 6:1, so too, the presence of sin does not give us permission to persist in sin. We are not trying to identify the point at which a believer, through persistent sin, can loose their salvation, or if that is a possibility. Jesus said we are His disciples if we "continue in His word", John 8: 31. If "whatsoever is not of faith is sin," Romans 14:23, then we could all be in trouble.

Demonization speaks of the amount of influence and control the evil one still holds in the saved person's life, just like sanctification speaks of the amount of area that has been liberated and is under the control of the Holy One. The area of a life still controlled, or occupied, by the enemy that has not yet been liberated by the Lamb and still demonized and unholy. Any part of the life given over to Christ and cleansed by his blood is holy ground. Yielding in an area through obedience to the Word brings that area under the control of the Holy Spirit and the covering of the Blood. Evil must move over, or out. The devil cannot stand on holy ground, ground bought with the precious Blood of the Lamb of God. We are comforted, "...knowing that [we] were not redeemed with corruptible things, like silver or gold, from [our] aimless conduct...but with the precious blood of Christ, as of a lamb without blemish and without spot." I Peter 1:18-19.

Deliverance is accomplished under only one circumstance, obedient surrender to the Lordship of Jesus Christ. Freedom may come as quiet repentance or in standing our ground against the devil. All deliverance is accomplished through and depends on obedience to the Word of God. The principles of control and ownership are both determined by that one thing. The Bible describes obedience as the one to whom we yield ourselves servant to obey; his slave we become. Romans 6:16. Jesus said, "...whoever commits sin is a slave of sin," John 8:34. If surrender determines the contest, obedience determines the surrender. Obedience rules the contest between God and Satan for the hearts of mankind. Control and conquest are determined not by God or Satan, but by us. Satan's plot is to deceive us into thinking, as he did with Adam and Eve, that we would be better off listening to him then God. The matter is simple after that. The one we obey becomes our master. We become his slave. Surrendering to Christ brings us into freedom because Jesus sets His slaves free and calls them sons and daughters.

It is not the Lord's will that rats are allowed to remain in His palace. Sanctification includes cleansing the temple of rats and debris. Restoration is accomplished by casting out demons and tearing down the strongholds of lies that have been built to undermine our faith in the Living God. As believers, God has given us the authority and command to set the rat traps and remove the rodents. The rats do not own the house, nor does their presence call into question the King's title to ownership. Their "possession" if you will, only extends to that part of the house they occupy, defile, and to some degree, control through their presence.

Garbage attracts rats. Where garbage accumulates, rats prosper. Some of that garbage is the legacy of sin inherited down through our generations. Some of it is our own doing, yielding to the flesh, that already unspiritually disposed part of us. God expects the believer to cooperate with His Spirit in the work of cleansing. The piles of garbage must be cleared out of our lives in order to prevent the breeding and feeding of the rats. But even as there is a connection between rats and garbage, there is a difference. Rats are personalities with design and intention. Garbage is the accumulated sin we have allowed to remain in our lives.

Garbage is the indulgence of the flesh, the heaps of debris that we, in our carnality, have allowed to remain in our lives and have learned to live with. The garbage accumulates when we fail to separate ourselves from our sin or haul it out and burn it on the altar of repentance. Jesus says to get rid of the garbage and it is best done daily. For some of us, the sanctification process simply means taking personal responsibility for our sin. We must stop making choices to indulge our carnal appetites and determine to make no provisions for the flesh.

For others, sanctification is more than just getting rid of the garbage. It may mean chasing out the rats. Getting rid of the garbage is not the same as killing a rat.

To kill a rat, we must go after them specifically with things that destroy rats. It takes more than a lip service, or a desire to be rid of the rodents. It takes poison, bullets, or gas to kill a rat. Rats in the King's Palace are driven out of the temple by the Blood of the Lamb, the Name of JESUS, and the Word of God, in declaration of Jesus as Lord.

Rats bring filth and embarrassment. Just as no one wants to admit they have rats in their house, people may be ashamed to speak of the strange movements, voices, or bizarre flashbacks they are feeling inside. The voices tell them they are crazy, or unredeemable. They are tormented with fear and loneliness, separated from a sound mind by racing thought and paranoia. They are the believers who live in condemnation and despair in need of a physician. Jesus came like a doctor, not to minister to those who are well, but to those who were sick. Jesus knew sickness could permeate a soul, a mind, or a spirit as surely as it can a body.

For some, part of the cleansing and sanctification process might include casting out of evil spirits. If Paul can talk about the "evil present within me", Romans 7: 21, can we not as correctly define that evil presence as an evil spirit? If that is true, what is that evil within us, that takes advantage of our sinful nature and predisposition if it is not an evil spirit? Evil is not a force without a purpose; it is a personality with a name and agenda. Just as Truth is embodied in the person of Jesus Christ, evil is contained in the person of the Devil. "For we do not wrestle against flesh and blood but against principalities, against powers, against the rulers of the darkness of this age, against spiritual hosts of wickedness in the heavenly places." Ephesians 6:12. This may seem like an over simplification of the situation, but there is no benefit to making things more complicated and complex than they really are.

20

LIGHT AND DARKNESS

Much discussion within the church on the subject of demonic activity in the believer has done little to help those believers whose problems seem to lie outside the parameters of acceptable behavior, as defined by tradition and church doctrine. Poor analogies that attest to the assumed impossibility of the duel occupation of light and darkness do not help. Some argue that light and darkness cannot inhabit the same place at the same time. At night, it is dark in my house any place where the lights are not turned on. When I turn on the light, however, things change. The light overrules the darkness wherever it finds it. That is the point. There are many rooms in the human heart. It is our choice to invite Christ to dwell in any or all of those rooms. He does not barge in to light every space at once, but where he is allowed to come in, the Light overcomes the darkness.

If we use the argument that light and darkness cannot be in the same place at the same time to refute the dual and simultaneous occupancy of God and the devil in the human life, we've missed the point. To insist that the argument proves that a Christian cannot have a demon is a serious breach of sound reason and a stretch of the analogy. To be defined as a Christian one must have opened himself up to the light of the Gospel. He has acknowledged his need for God in his life. We come to Christ because we have been drawn. He was not restricted or repulsed from His initial workings in our life because of our dark and awful past. The darkness could not prevent the light from coming in, any more than the night can prevent the dawn. The process of sanctification is letting the light in as determined by our continued willingness to trust and obey the Lord and His Word.

If Satan physically prowled around in the court of heaven to banter with God about Job, do we wonder that he still petitions God to afflict contemporary believers on earth? The argument that light and darkness cannot mingle is not sufficient to answer all the questions and conditions that are raised in the actual experience in a believer's life. Not only is the analogy that light and darkness cannot mix or abide in the same place at the same time a poor analogy for explaining the difficult spiritual truths of demonization; they are unscientific as well. Darkness is always present in the same place as light. When the light comes in it overpowers the darkness, therefore, we do not experience the darkness. When the light is taken away, no one has to turn on the darkness because it is just there. To draw the conclusion that God and the devil cannot be in the same place, i.e., human vessel, at the same time, is to deny Satan's coming before the Lord as recorded in the book of Job. It would mean we must also deny that the pure sinless Son of God lived for 33 years on a planet governed by the prince of the darkness.

DRIFTERS IN THE SWAMP

How can demons live in a Christian's life? The same way drifters can live in a swamp on the back forty of a plantation. Imagine your life is like a farm or a plantation. The farmer lives in the "house on the hill." His land is divided into various fields and pastures, some tillable and some, unproductive. The cultivated areas are well developed and watched over. The other areas may be not only less productive, but left untended for weeks or years at a time, as is often the case with marsh lands, swamps and bogs. Consider what would happen if, in the absence of the farmer, these areas began to be occupied with drifters or vagabonds. They could go unnoticed for a long time, taking advantage of the opportunity to build up their unscrupulous influence and illegal use of the farmer's land. The trespassers' occupation of the property though not legal, would be actual. Their intention to homestead could include setting up a permanent camp, shooting the rabbits, chopping down the trees, putting up a temporary lean-to and planting a little garden. And if that is not enough of an intrusion, they have the audacity to invite more from their wandering company to settle down and stay.

From their perspective, everything is nice as long as their activities are unnoticed. They have got the run of the place and they love it. No one really bothers them and soon they have built a little city of unauthorized undisturbed drifters. If possession, (occupation) is nine/tenths of the law, then these fellows have it with their eye on more. Isn't that just like the devil? He'll keep on grabbing and digging until someone stops him. The Lord says it is time to stop the pillaging and restore, reclaim and rebuild the kingdom.

Now, we can choose to ignore the problem or we may be unaware of it all together. Neither of these conditions prevent the continued stripping of resources or erosion of the land. Satan is busy carrying off the assets of the farmer's soul, working diligently toward the day when he can tie him up and take complete control of the farm.

All goes as planned until Jesus purchases the property. He comes into a life and takes up residence in the house on the hill. He lives with the farmer and intends to put a stop to the destruction. He does this by giving the land owner His authority to repossess the ground and make the land productive. He shows him how to increase its productivity. "He gave them power over unclean spirits, to cast them out...," Matthew 10:1. He has come to help us redeem the waste places and reclaim the swamps of our lives.

"I have given you authority to trample on serpents and scorpions and over all the power of the enemy and nothing shall by any means hurt you." Luke 10:19-20. The works get done as we step out in faith and go down into the swamps and speak God's truth into the strongholds of our lives. The devil doesn't own us and we don't owe him anything. He doesn't pay the rent or taxes. The Blood of Jesus paid our debt to justice and purchased the property free and clear. The only thing left to do is bring the land into full productivity for His kingdom's sake.

DEADLY ASSUMPTIONS

Our misunderstanding of the simple principles, ownership and occupancy have made us vulnerable to the lies of the destroyer and opened our door to the thief. To deny the truth is to embrace the lie. The enemy has even used us against each other. He keeps us in bondage to our assumptions and delights in sewing discord and division to isolate individual believers. Some of us choose willful ignorance, thinking we cannot have a problem because we are saved. Others of us dare not mention our secret fears about the presence of the enemy in our lives, concerned about what others will say or think. Our salvation and our sincerity might be called into question.

Even though we are moving into a more outspoken generation that talks about what has been hidden in closets for lifetimes, we are still uncomfortable about things we do not understand. It is easier to believe someone is not really saved, than to think they could be saved and demonized. We judge by appearance, and draw incorrect conclusions. It is wonderfully true that if any man is in Christ, he (she) is a new creature. "Old things pass away and behold, all things become new," II Corinthians 5:17, but all of the character defects, short comings and personality flaws do not just melt away like old snow on a warm spring day. The truth of being a new creature in Christ is at first and by far more apparent in the heavenly realm than it is for the still earth-bound believer. We do not want to make the deadly assumption that what I do not know cannot hurt me, or what I cannot see is not really there, or that coming to Christ is an instant and painless process. Coming into the "all things become new" experience is a process called sanctification that lasts a lifetime and costs us everything. From the moment of rebirth until the believer is welcomed home into glory the exchange of death for life continues.

OWNERSHIP ON ALL THREE COUNTS

We have discussed ownership and occupation, but what about openings? As new creatures in Christ, God legitimately establishes His ownership of us on three counts. He created us, He redeemed us, and now, in the act of salvation, we gave Him our lives. He made us, bought us and we've given Him our hearts as a gift. The enemy gets things by stealing and laying false claim to them. At the Fall when Adam and Eve forfeited the dominion and management of their garden estate, they too became property of the one they obeyed. With their surrender to the lie, the devil got everything that belonged to them, including their offspring. They were stripped of their freedom and shackled with death.

Paul reflects that condition in Romans 7: 15, 17, & 18-21 where he writes " For what I am doing, I do not understand. For what I will to do, that I do not practice; but what I hate, that I do. But now, it is no longer I who do it, but sin that dwells in me. For the good that I will to do, I do not do; but the evil I will not to do, that I practice. Now if I do what I will not to do, it is no longer I who do it, but sin that dwells in me." He concludes the conflict comes from the "sin that dwells in me." Verse 21 calls it the "evil present within." I find than a law, that evil is present with me, the one who wills to do good." How did the evil get in, and if that is true, is there any hope for goodness to prevail in our lives?

LIONS IN THE LIVING ROOM

Evil gained access through the original sin of our first parents and has continued as the default ever since.

25

The enemy enlarged the breach and continues to gets in through the doorways. Why would the devil scale a wall when he could use a doorway, one which in many cases has already been opened. In many of our lives, the doors are so open they have fallen off their hinges. Doors are opened through sin and have been left hanging open through neglect, from one generation to the next through unrepentance and carelessness. We have failed to realize how extremely vulnerable we are to the devil. He goes about as a roaring lion, seeking whom he may devour and we become an easy prey.

If all we had to do to protect ourselves was to get up and shut the door, we would be foolish not to. When we realize how easy it would have been to shut the door and restrain the evil that operates in our lives, we would be appalled and ashamed that we have neglected doing it sooner. Failing to apply the simple truth of God's Word to our needs has become an even greater tragedy than the original condition itself.

Living with a lion in the living room of our life is not necessary, nor is it a safe environment in which to nurture our life. Instead of security and sense of well-being, we are torn up with alcohol, divorce, abuse, greed and every other form of ravaging the evil spirits can bring to bear. For too many of us, the doors have been left open for generations and no one bothers to get up to shut them. The effects of our complacency have left our children battered, and mauled. Some of them have been devoured, eaten up by sin and devastated by the effects of the enemy's presence in their lives. They spend much, if not all of their adult lives trying to make sense of or put to rest, or get free from, the things that happened to them in childhood. The lion is no respecter of persons. The lives of children of even well-intentioned parents have been strewn with defeat, misery and misfortunes.

Somehow the enemy has succeeded in convincing

us that he has won and the victim role is the only part left for us to play. We believe we are doomed to remain bound to the despair and frustration of the past. Some might think their misfortune is a stroke of bad luck or fate. If that were the case, we would have to suppose things that happened to us were arbitrary and without a cause. Application of God's Words to the wounds of the heart and mind still brings help, hope and healing if we are willing to hear them. Christ has called us to be more than conquerors. He sees us to be victors. By God's grace and through His guidance, we still have time to do this thing right and become free to make a difference in somebody else's life.

CHAPTER TWO

BRING FORTH YOUR STRONG REASONS IS. 41:21

TRUTH = FREEDOM

For the believer to be able to proceed with confidence against the work of the enemy in their lives, it is essential to understand the scriptural rational for the principles of truth, obedience, ownership and freedom. The principles of God's Word are firmly planted at the root of all human experience. "You shall know the truth and the truth shall set you free", John 8:32. Rewritten as a mathematical equation this scripture would read: Truth = Freedom. [By definition, if the opposite of truth is the lie, and the opposite of freedom is bondage.] Therefore, using the mathematical property of opposites, definitions, and the transitive property, we can conclude: If Truth = Freedom, then by the definition of opposites, Lies = Bondage. It must be true, then, that if freedom comes from truth, bondage must come from lies. If lies bring us into bondage, then it is correct to conclude that a person living in bondage and oppression, must be believing lies. Conversely, if we read the equation, Truth = Freedom, we know that a believer who is walking in freedom is walking in truth.

THE CURSE WITHOUT A CAUSE

Proverbs 26:2 says "the curse without a cause does not come." Scientific logic reinterprets that to mean that there is a reason for the curse, and that the evil we see ravaging people's lives is the result of a cause. If there is a cause, what is it? Understanding that curses have causes establishes the orderliness, reason, and deliberate actions of a purposeful God. He does not randomly allow evil or bad things to come. This is good news. God is in control. The

28

come by coincidence or at the hand of fate. God's truth protects those who surrender to it. We are not at the mercy of a merciless devil. God's plan that we overcome our adversary and walk in victory is a plan for all believers, not just a select few.

Given the idea of the presence and personification of evil makes it easy to make a strong case for documenting the source of many of our contemporary ills both as a society, and individually. Psalms 107:10-11 talks about "those who sat in darkness and in the shadow of death, bound in affliction and irons – because they rebelled against the words of God, and despised the counsel of the Most High". Jeremiah 5:25 says "Your iniquities have turned these things, (the rains and harvest) away, and your sins have withheld good from you."

OBEDIENCE AND BLESSING

Obedience to God activates blessings. Disobedience opens the door to the oppressor. Whom you yield yourself servant to obey, his slave you become, is the rule of ownership and servitude for both the kingdom of good and evil. Obedience to God is called righteousness. Consistent obedience to God brings deliverance. Obedience to Satan is called sin. Our consent to either God or Satan gives them permission to operate in and have access to those parts of us involved in the act. Romans 6:12-13 says, "Therefore do not let sin reign in your mortal body, that you should obey it in its lusts. Do not present your members as instruments of unrighteousness to sin, but present yourselves to God as being alive from the dead, and your members as instruments of righteousness to God."

Our disobedience to God ties His hand of blessing in our lives and opens the door to the enemy, making us the prize of evil. The chosen people, Abraham's descendents thought the inheritance and right to the Promised Land should be theirs automatically, without qualification. The

Lord corrected their thinking in Ezekiel 33:23-28. "Son of man, they who inhabit those ruins in the land of Israel are saying, 'Abraham was only one, and he inherited the land. But we are many; the land has been given to us as a possession'." God goes on to describe their sins of eating blood, lifting up their eyes to idols and shedding blood as an abomination. "Should you then possess the land?" He asks. He adds more sins to the list and declares emphatically, "As I live, surely those who are in the ruins shall fall by the sword...be devoured by beasts...die in caves...then they shall know that I am the Lord when I have made the land most desolate." Sin brings judgment and destroys both the heirs and the inheritance.

Deuteronomy is full of the "if-then" conditions for blessings and curses. We can draw clear and direct conclusions from such strongly worded passages as Deuteronomy 30:11-20. "For this commandment which I command you today, it is not too mysterious for you, nor is it far off." Verse 15 says, "See, I have set before you today life and good, death, evil, in that I command you today to love the Lord your God, to walk in His ways, and keep His commandments...that you may live and multiply; and the Lord your God will bless you...But if your heart turns away,...I announce to you today that you shall surely perish...I have set before you life and death, blessing and cursing; therefore choose life that both you and your descendants may live."

Disobedience and yielding to Satan gives him legal right to set up a place, a foothold in our lives; "...nor give place to the devil," Ephesians 4:27. From that foothold, he works to establish a stronghold. The Bible declares the sins of the generations are visited onto the children to the third and fourth generations. Exodus 20:5 says, "For I the Lord, your God, am a jealous God, visiting the iniquity of the fathers on the children to the third and fourth generations of those who hate Me, but showing mercy to thousands who love Me and keep My commandments."

Our protest that these are scriptures of the Old Testament must include the fact that the "I Am" God of the Old Testament is the same God in the New Testament. "He is the same, yesterday, today, and forever," Hebrews 13:8. He is the same. His standards have not changed. The Old Testament serves as a type or foreshadowing of the spiritual realities found and fulfilled in Jesus Christ in the New Testament.

In light of that connection, we find that the principles as foreshadowed in the Old Testament are so steadfast and sure that they can be used to identify the patterns of blessing and cursing that are operating in a New Testament life. The pattern of both good and bad in a believer's life is predictable and replicated from one generation to the next with such accuracy that even the similarities in the original ages and places are repeated in the successive generations.

A NEW CREATURE

The Bible says that "if any man is in Christ, he is a new creature, old things pass away, behold all things are new," II Corinthians 5: 17. God wants the old patterns of sin and destruction destroyed through the establishment of the new inheritance. The new creature of II Corinthians 5:17 is as true as the sanctification process that the new creature must go through as described in II Corinthians 7:1. We are called to "cleanse ourselves from all filthiness of the flesh and spirit, perfecting holiness in the fear of God." Salvation is an event, a birth. Sanctification is a process, a lifetime. Being seated in heavenly places spiritually in Christ Jesus, Ephesians. 1:20, as a reality, does not diminish the realities of sitting in the middle of a traffic jam in rush hour. Reality runs true on at least two levels of

31

experience simultaneously, with neither being any less true or diminished by the existence of the other.

How can we be seated with Christ and still be experiencing incredible setbacks and opposition in the natural world? The Bible says in I John 5:4, "For whatever is born of God overcomes the world. And this is the victory that has overcome the world – our faith." Jesus said He came that "they might have life and life more abundantly," John 10:10. But where is that abundant life? Many Christians are as oppressed and overrun as unbelievers. They suffer from the same ongoing effects of sins and are caught in consequences of sins as unbelievers, snared in the consequences of sin they have not even committed themselves.

THE WASHING MACHINE THEORY

It would be nice if the washing machine theory of salvation were true. We could throw sinners into the laundry tub of salvation and lift out shiny white saints. That could be true except for the fact that the apostles give us some of the strongest examples of post-salvation, bad behavior recorded in scriptures. On more than one occasion, Jesus had to correct them for their unbelief and selfish ambition, their quarreling and self-righteous judgments. Jesus recognized the need for sanctification and told Peter to strengthen his brethren after he got converted himself.

Salvation is a free gift that calls us to surrender everything we have in terms of pursuit and ambition that we might be one hundred percent fruitful. Salvation is not an easy answer or a quick fix to life's problems. Asking Jesus to take over the strongholds of darkness, in reality, is a declaration of war, not peace. Salvation means being birthed into the family of God. Birth does not provide education but opportunity for education. Faulty thinking wants us to believe asking God into our hearts is enough to do the job and automatically gets the devils out. Where in the natural world is that true? Even a tree lies where it falls. Problems left untreated don't go away. They compound, and often grow worse. The children of Israel could not just ignore the giants in the Promised Land, nor did the giants offer to pack up and leave when they heard the children of the inheritance were back.

PRE-SET TO SIN

I John 3: 6 says, "Whoever abides in Him does not sin." "Walk in the Spirit and you shall not fulfill the lusts of the flesh", Galatians 5:16. How do we reconcile those scriptures? How do we account for Paul's dilemma in Romans 7 of doing those things he didn't want to do and not doing those things he believed to be right? Sin is like the default mode on the computer. The flesh is the pre-set on the human disposition. We are born pre-programmed to sin and destruction. This doesn't mean we do not have a free will. The PC owner has a choice to allow the computer to function under the default, or take one of the other options made available on the display menu. If no choice is made, the default functions to control the computer's choice of operation.

We function under a similar set of rules. The flesh is pre-set to sin. Dogs bark, fish swim, sinners sin. That is just the way it is. It is the natural course of events. All have sinned and come short of the glory of God. The flesh is our predisposition and tendency toward sin. Flesh is our combined flaws and weaknesses. Flesh is the fallen nature in need of redemption. Sin is the default on the hard-drive. Unless we realize our options to walk in the Spirit and change the default, we will not experience any of the changes Christ desires we should enjoy as His redeemed. God's Word does not return to Him void or fruitless, but accomplishes His Will wherever it is sent.

The Word of God is intended to bring forth new life in us by giving us a revelation of Jesus Christ, the Truth. His truth acts as light to dispel the darkness and do a work of righteousness in us. All have sinned and come short of the Glory of God. Our predisposition and tendency toward sin gives our flesh the advantage. It is the first choice. To act against it we must make a deliberate choice to do differently. Unless we realize our options to walk in the Spirit and change the default, we will not experience any of the changes or freedoms Christ desires we should enjoy as His redeemed.

SIN IS NOT THE PROBLEM

It is also important to understand that sin is not the problem here. Sin is the product and result of believing lies about God's goodness and His faithfulness. When the serpent tempted Eve he reasoned against the good intentions of God. Eve's confidence in the integrity of God began to falter. Doubt told her she could be wrong. Her belief about God might not be right. Her sin was in allowing a lie to take the place of the truth. That lie then led to the eating of the forbidden fruit, the act of sin. Sin is the result of acting on our unbelief. Unbelief has to do with rejecting or not believing the truth. The problem then, is not sin but the lie behind the sin. Sin is the outcome of believing lies. It is not sin that binds us in the devil's strongholds but the lies we believe. Lies are the opposite of truth. Lies are the only thing the devil can use to bind us to the sin because lies are all he has. Jesus called him the father of lies, John 8:44. Because lies are the only, always and forever thing the devil uses to bind us, truth belongs to and is essential to God's nature. Truth is the only, always and forever thing that can set us free. The problem then is in not believing the truth. Every trial and temptation to sin is a test of faith that can be distilled into one simple question. Do we believe God? Do we believe His Word or

34

the circumstances pressing in around us? Every trial is a test of trust.

If we try to eradicate the sin from our lives by simply trying harder to be good, we only become frustrated, religious and exhausted. No one is good enough to go to heaven and no one goes to hell because they are bad. We go to heaven because we have accepted Jesus Christ as our Savior. We go to hell because we have rejected Him. Anything more or less then this is an exercise in pride and religious futility. We will fall into the same trap of legalism, which the Pharisees fell into, and we will be judged with the same judgment with which we judged them.

The power of the enemy's strategy to destroy is subtle and often overlooked. Satan chains us to a lie by convincing us that we must purge ourselves of our own sin by being good or perfect. This is the favorite past time of religious spirits. The possibilities for paranoia and anxiety are endless. Division and fragmentation result in confusion and doublemindedness. Set in perpetual motion by the lie to pursue our own righteousness, we never stop long enough to realize the insidious plot against us. We end up failing, frustrated in our efforts to establish our own righteousness. We are deceived by religious spirits and angels of light impersonating the Spirit. They pass off a dead form of godliness and the letter of the law as coming from the Spirit of liberty and truth. In believing our lies, we have become more bound by Satan than any criminal ever sent to Alcatraz. The devil has locked us in a prison where the walls are lies as "thin as air" but as real as if they were the Rock of Gibraltar.

If sin is like the leaves and fruit, then the lies we believe are the root and stem of the evil tree. The lies are planted in the tender soil of the unsuspecting, watered and reinforced by the misinterpretation of experiences, and cared for by the wicked one, until the deadly fruit appears.

We eat the poisonous fruit and become spiritually weak, even sick unto death. We can pick off leaves and fruit until we are "blue in the face" and still fall short of His righteousness. Our only hope is to get to the root. Jesus said, "whom the Son sets free is free indeed," John 8:36. He came that we might have life and life more abundantly, not that we could eat poison and call ourselves survivors.

We cannot make ourselves righteous any more then the nation of Israel could keep the Commandments. God does not ask us to make ourselves righteous, He only commands us to OBEY. The challenge to the flesh is to obey the directives of the Holy Spirit who is given to us to lead us into all TRUTH. The truth only comes from the Holy Spirit as He gives us a REVELATION of Jesus Christ. That revelation of TRUTH is what sets us free from the bondage of the lie, and destroys death, the fruit of sin.

TRUTH IS THE KEY TO DELIVERANCE

Knowing the truth is the key to deliverance, inner healing and freedom for the believer. That deliverance sometimes looks like healing for the body, as well. Many times the oppression in the soul, the mind, will and emotions, have created physical pain and dysfunction in the body as well. Mysterious pains for which the doctors cannot find an organic reason are often the result of spiritual and emotional attacks. Often the enemy works from the inside out to bring complete dysfunction to the life. What better way to reap the full benefit of the lies then to incapacitate us who are the "fearfully and wonderfully made" reflections of the image of God?

Many of God's sons and daughters are defeated, overcome by fear and doubt. They are held hostage in their own souls, hidden away as prisoners of war in their own lives, held captive by the lies they believe are truth. It is time we stop denying the obvious and get up and fight. This is war whether we want to believe it or not. God's Word is the textbook on spiritual warfare that gives us the strategy for setting the captives free. It gives clear admonition to rescue those drawn to death, Proverbs 24: 11-12. It lays out with consistency and accuracy, if not in detail, at least in principle, the solution to every human condition and experience. "The weapons of our warfare are not carnal, but mighty to the pulling down of strongholds," II Corinthians 10:4. The truths of God's Word become dynamic and powerful when they are specific. The challenge to Christian life and discipleship is to teach and apply these truths skillfully to the specific conditions of our lives.

God's Word is full of instruction to bring us into the knowledge of the truth. It is our sword and our strategy to defeat the devil. It contains the battle plan for taking back from Satan the things that rightfully belong to the believer. Jesus began that work when He confronted Satan in the wilderness and finished it when He descended into the belly of hell. He stripped the devil of the keys of hell and death and reinstated Adam and Eve as rightful heirs to Heaven.

He has commissioned us to continue to press the enemy until His Kingdom comes and His Father's will is done, on the earth as it is in heaven..., Matthew 6:9-13. We will not accomplish the task by legalistically legislating the eradication of sin, but by bringing the Light of the Gospel to those whom are sitting in the pits and prison houses of inner darkness. God's Word will not return to Him void and fruitless. It accomplishes His will wherever it is sent and whenever it is applied in faith.

CHAPTER THREE

BELIEF SYSTEMS: THE TRUTH VS. THE LIE

BELIEFS DETERMINED BY EXPERIENCE

When we form our beliefs, we make the assumption they are true. Whether they actually are true or not is immaterial in regard to the power we give them. Once we believe something is true, it begins to rule and influence and control our decisions.

Our beliefs both come out of our experiences, and create our experiences. We interpret the things that happen to us in the context of past experiences. Our beliefs are critical to the discussion of healing because they not only tell us about our past, but are powerful predictors of our future. What we believe is critical to our health and wholeness because truth is the foundation of our freedom and authority in God.

Over time, beliefs solidify into mindsets that fossilize into stone towers of tradition. A stone tower can be a place of safety or a prison, depending on who keeps the tower and how it is used. Once our belief towers are built, they are not likely to be further challenged by us or look much different from the towers of our generations past out of which we gathered the stones.

If our beliefs are not in accurate agreement with the Word of God, collectively and individually, they assemble to form the assumptions, false doctrine, and deep rooted prejudices; the "great" darkness Jesus talked about in Matthew 6:23, "If therefore the light that is in you is darkness, how great is that darkness!" They provide the openings for error the enemy uses to invade our lives.

THE POTTER'S PART

A lump of clay is a lump of clay. It acts like clay, and lies like clay. It cannot be anything else, because it is clay. It responds to the hand of the potter and his wheel as he uses the properties of the clay to mold its potential into a specific vessel. The gifts and abilities inborn and unique to us can be shaped and developed in either a positive or a negative way, by the potters who raise us. The identity we form comes much from the design and intention of the potters who touch us day after day. Both their care and neglect can clearly be seen reflected in the final product. The things they teach us through example and the things we learn about ourselves from them, come together to shape our behavior and philosophy of life. The information we gathered as children become foundational for the things we come to believe, be they truth or error.

GATHERING MY IDENTITY

Many of our beliefs are fashioned in our childhood. The tasks of evaluating and categorizing experiences and forming concepts are made by children who cannot yet even keep their rooms cleaned or remember to brush their teeth without adult supervision. If foolishness is bound in the heart of a child, Proverbs 22:15, then it stands to reason, that some of the conclusions we formed as children, are foolish and unrealistic and in desperate need of re-evaluation.

Powerful but subtle lies often form the foundation of our behavior and our relationships. To believe that everyone must love me in order for me to be lovable is unrealistic. To believe that everyone can be trusted is dangerous. To believe that the world revolves around me is immature and narcissistic. To think that if I am beaten and abused by those around me I am bad and to blame, is foolish. To a young child who carries an innate sense of two things; my parents are good and can do no wrong, and

I am the center and cause of the things around me, these ideas are perfectly reasonable conclusions. As untrue and unrealistic as these conclusions are, children believe them. The folly is magnified when, as adults, many of us still continue to believe we are the main problem or the only solution to the difficulties we face, and that our opinions order the universe.

We make the assumption that everything we believe to be true is true. Many of our ideas have never undergone formal review in our adulthood or been measured against the Word of God. Just because we believe something does not automatically make it accurate or correct. How much more the case, for things I concluded as a five year old?

Much of the bondage and dissatisfaction in our lives comes from the fact that we do not know the truth about our identity or our authority in Christ. In our gullibility, we have chosen to believe Satan's pronouncements over us, rather than the words of the Father. "For I know the thoughts that I think toward you, says the Lord, thoughts of peace and not of evil, to give you a future and a hope." Jeremiah 29:11. God is good. His plan for us is to experience life, and "life more abundantly," John 10:10. "I have given you authority"..."over all the power of the enemy and nothing shall by any means hurt you," Luke 10:19.

We have "exchanged the truth of God for the lie," Romans 1:25, and became confined by the lies we have believed. We have allowed them to define our identity and the world in which we live. The fortresses these beliefs have created are much more substantial than we want to believe. We lose our courage to change and believe that our beliefs cannot be changed. "That's just the way I am," we explain. We lose sight of our uniqueness as created in the image of God. Our thinking has become clouded and so immersed in the lies of the devil that we have a hard time separating ourselves from him or believing we can

40

change.

Many of the ideas we've gathered about ourselves have come from those around us. Our parents, teachers, and peers have all left their impressions. From them we've gathered information about our likability and abilities. We determine our value by the worth others ascribe to us. We calculate our value from the time and interest other people have been willing to invest in our lives. If they are unwilling to spend time with us, if they hurt us deliberately or neglect us carelessly, we conclude we are inferior and unlovable. Much of the information we use to create our impressions of ourselves is skewed, if not misconstrued altogether. Our primary beliefs become malicious and self-destructive making us vulnerable to the enemy's attack.

Often the information communicated to us comes from parents, siblings, peers and other significant people in our childhood who are in error themselves. Subconsciously we begin to respond to words that are not true as the enemy uses these key powerful people in our life, whether they realize it or not. We tend to develop and define our personal view of ourselves based on the opinions of others because our identity does not come preformed or prebuilt from the factory of heaven. We are not born cut in stone, but etched in sand. We become what we are told, believing it to be true. When we believe the truth of God, we become like a piece of fine marble in the Master's hand. If we do not believe God, our lives are like driftwood permeated with holes strewn haplessly along the shores of life.

THE FOURTH LITTLE PIG

Believing is powerful. What we believe forms the essential material from which we build our "Self" concept. The words and deeds of others become the materials out of which we construct our self-image. If the same is true of piglets, the story of the Three Little Pigs might go something like this.

Once upon a time there were three little pigs. The first little pig was almost grown and about to leave home. His parents did what they could, but they were themselves busy and often distracted with their own pursuits. They often gave into little piglet's wants and wishes, giving him few guidelines with which to govern his life. The straw that they gave him was soft and slippery and seemed easy to work with. Soon the first little pig had his house built. It looked nice from the outside, a great place where he could kick back and relax, and he was confident in his work. But no sooner had he sat down when the wolf came thundering his threats. "I'm going to huff and puff, and blow your house down!" Alas, the first little pig's poor foundation and false security held for him no real or lasting safety, and he was destroyed. His life had been built with materials that were not strong or solid enough to weather the storms of life.

When the second little pig left home, he was confident that his talent and accomplishments would see him through. He had been given a large bundle of strong sticks with which to build his house and he was eager to get started on his life. He worked with religious fervor, trusting the tried and trusted traditions of his instructors, believing he key to success was tucked safely in his pocket. His parents were proud of him and he was sure he had what it took to beat the wolf. But, alas, the wolf came calling more then ready to take on the challenge. He huffed and he puffed, and after a little while, the second little pig stumbled and fell into depression and took his own life.

The third little pig was more fortunate. He had learned from the first two little pigs. His parents and the people in his life gave him bricks with which to build. They came and helped him lay strong foundations of truth and walls of integrity. When the wolf heard of it he was not impressed and thought for sure he would have this little pig too. But there was one big difference. This little pig had used beliefs and values that would stand the test of truth that protected him from the ferocious howling of the wolf. Though he huffed and puffed with all his might, the wolf could not destroy the little pig or what he had build.

Now, this would make a nice ending and we all like those kinds of endings, and that is why little is told of the fourth little pig. He was a more modern day child whose parents were preoccupied with their own problems and addictions. Some of these parents comforted themselves with drugs and pleasure. Others avoid responsibilities of parenting by holding on to their own pain. They were too distracted and disinterested to give their little piglet anything with which to build his life, so he used what he could find on his own; old rotten boards, rusty nails, cardboard and broken pieces of glass. He was neglected and treated like a throwaway, left to his own survival devices. He felt unvalued and saw his life with disdain. He would have to build his house out of the broken promises, abusive words, temporary escapes and acts of self-preservation and violence he had collected. He worked alone, and I must admit, he was angry and bitter, which didn't help much, considering the seriousness of the task. It was no wonder he left home early and chose to live for a time, in the street with his gang family. Homelessness didn't seem that inconvenient and building a house was not a priority. He had no identity, so it was no wonder his attention was absorbed in pain reduction and his conscience was ill formed. His life could be summed up like so many of today's children who live trying to pet the wolf.

FALSE TRUTH IS GREAT DARKNESS
Every time we accept the devil's lie, we give him permission to use it to build his stronghold in our lives. The lies we believe create mindsets. The enemy uses the mindset to influence our decisions. Believing the lie is sin against the truth of God. Our decision to pursue the lie,

(sin), eventually forms a behavior. From that behavior, we begin to make statements about our identity and ourselves. We hear the lies we are telling ourselves and receive the lies as true. We act on this false truth and the vicious cycle of failure and lies goes around again. We see the behavior which results from these actions. We read our behavior as us acting in accordance with who we are. Who we are grows into who we become. We have defined ourselves by the sin we see ourselves doing and come to believe we are the evil we do.

The only way to break the cycle and get set free of the enemy's grip on our mind is to let go of the lie. This is easier said than done, because over the course of time the lie and the self have merged into what we call our identity. Getting rid of the lie takes more then pasting paper sticky notes to the bathroom mirror reminding me to tell myself "I am beautiful." Letting go cannot be done by doing more or by doing different. Letting go of the lie is a severing process accomplished when we receive God's truth into our life on that specific issue. Only truth can neutralize the lie and make it ineffective.

AS A MAN THINKS IN HIS HEART

Proverbs 23:9 says, "as [a man] thinks in his heart so he is." The heart of the miser says, "eat and drink,"…but his heart is not with you. What we believe in our hearts defines who we are. Out of the abundance of the Heart the mouth speaks," Matthew 12:34. Our heart is the seat of our affections and the source of our true feelings. Our true feelings and fears come from the values and beliefs the heart holds. True healing and hope cannot come until Jesus Christ, the great heart surgeon, comes to remove the lies that bind and break the heart. When He reveals His truth about a matter, freedom comes and pain goes. What is impossible to accomplish with reason and good sense and persuasion and intellectual assent is quickly accomplished by the other one who was there to witness the original event, and the only one who can go back to fix it. Jesus moves as easily into the past as He does in the present and the future. They are all the same to Him because eternity is a circle of time, not a line. God is not limited to just going forward in time. He is present in the past as much as He abides with us in the present. Only He can go back in time and heal a broken heart, or liberate us from the hold of the lie and give peace to a painful memory.

Letting go of the lie is as simple as accepting God's view on the event. We do not have to deny the truth or continue to bear the burden of the sins of others committed against us. Jesus offers His truth unconditionally and encourages us to take it. Truth is the only thing that can set us free from the pain in our heart and loose us from the grief in our memories. When the truth comes in, the lie is exposed and pain leaves. The only truth is the truth Jesus tells. That which was believed was really a lie built to look true. The only truth about it was the chain it built to put around our neck to destroy us.

It is true that "in my flesh no good thing dwells", but it's also true that we are created in the image of God Himself. Genesis 1:26. We fail to see that the thing that dwells along with us in our flesh is often the presence of evil itself. It is a spirit sent from the enemy to take advantage of our ignorance and to seize upon our soul. If the house of "self" is not built in truth, we become vulnerable and doomed to destruction.

HARMLESS IS DEADLY

Many of the words and beliefs we pick up seem small and harmless at first, but they grow. Silently, in the darkness of the child's mind they develop into the thoughts that begin to rule the child's actions. The power of the words can be seen in the self-fulfilling prophecies they produce. Nicknames and labels have the power to bring forth reality. Beliefs that began not as truth, but as a word, become truth to us. "You are stupid" may start out as a harsh comment made by a frustrated parent, and end up becoming our own opinion of ourselves. We begin to believe the lies and accept the things we do as stupid.

WHAT DO YOU BELIEVE?

The beliefs we hold about God, the world, family, my purpose and me become the foundational concepts that our minds use to make decisions and activate behaviors. These concepts are built, like any other structure, line upon line and precept upon precept, Isaiah 28:10-13. As the Bible describes it. "If the foundations are destroyed, what can the righteous do?" Psalms 11:3. Our own version of truth forms the foundation for life, but our belief systems are often left unexamined and unreconciled with the Word of God. Romans 12:1-2 says "to be transformed by the renewing of your mind." The renewal of the mind is a process of exchanging the lie for the truth.

ABOUT GOD'S WORD

To understand and believe that truth is found unequivocally in the Word of God is essential to successful Christian living. To function as a productive member among the company of the redeemed, we must embrace God's Word as the standard. His Word sets forth the basic principles that undergird our authority as ambassadors to earth, and empowers us as believers, to enforce the victory of the resurrection. The truth of God's Word, when strategically applied, defeats the specific strongholds of pain and oppression held by the enemy in our lives. Believing what the Word says allows us to operate in the truth. Understanding the legal basis for our authority is crucial to moving with confidence against the enemy, and fundamental in obtaining the freedom and power we seek to defeat him and take back what he has stolen from us.

God's Word is the first and final authority on every matter. His mercy rules within the parameter of His justice. His truth brings freedom. Self-determination does not. His life lived in us gives us purpose. Any other life or power living in us brings us into bondage and death. If Satan can convince us that God is unjust or uncaring, whom can we turn to? If God abandons us and marks iniquities without a place of reconciliation, we are all doomed to a life worse than this present bondage.

Until we accept things as God says they are, including who we are, we will live in the lie. We will live our lives in the shadow because we have refused the light of God's truth. Not accepting God's Word prevents the truth from coming into our lives to set us free. Without a firm belief in His Word as totally accurate and absolutely reliable, we do not even enter the arena, let alone contest the enemy. If the devil can keep us double minded in this, he can keep us in deception. We are helpless against his lie without the truth. He is a thief who works best in the shadow, lurking in places where we are confused and in denial. He hopes to ultimately steal from us our most precious possession, our soul. If we do not guard those things precious to us and hold the truth close to our heart, he will come with his lie. For that reason, we must "take every thought captive," II Corinthians 10:5, and lay it up against the standard, and make it line up with the "obedience of Christ."

ABOUT GOD

What do we believe to be true about God? If we see Him as too busy or uninterested or angry, we will have a hard time experiencing His goodness and love. The devil uses every opportunity he can to reinforce the lies he has planted in our lives. "See, you prayed, and nothing happened. Now doesn't that just go to show you God doesn't care about you?" "If God is so powerful, why did He let this happen?" "Where is God when you really need Him?"

If I think it all depends on my super faith, and me or that I am sufficient in myself, I will become arrogant and proud. If being perfect is important to me, I will become rigid and religious. Many of us are wrapped in religious practices, steeped in the form of godliness, not even aware of our denying the power of it. If my concept of why I am here is to have a good time, I will have a hard time living my life as a bondservant to Jesus Christ. If I believe the devil is just a comic strip creation, or a good costume idea for a Halloween party, I will not resist him with any determination, nor will I see that he is robbing me blind.

ABOUT GOD'S WILL

What is God's will and desire for us? Jesus said, " I am come that you might have life and life more abundantly," John 10:10. He has come to give us "for the spirit of heaviness; "beauty for ashes, oil of joy for mourning, the garment of praise" Isaiah 61:3a.

"If any man is in Christ, he is a new creature," II Corinthians 5:17. He came to " ...heal the brokenhearted, preach deliverance to the captives, recovery of sight to the blind, and set at liberty the oppressed," Isaiah 61:1. Jesus came to minister healing and hope, a continuation of the Father's desire to bless His people and prepare a Bride for His Son.

The Father warned in Deuteronomy 4:40, to keep His commandments... "that it may go well with you and your children after you,...that you may prolong your days." He warned them not to make carved images, in Deuteronomy 5:8-10 because He was a "jealous God, visiting the iniquity of the fathers on to the children." Deuteronomy 7:11 promises that He will love and bless those who keep the commandments, and listen to His judgments.   He promises to multiply them and their offspring and flocks, and take away barrenness, sickness and terrible diseases. God's desires to bless and shower us with Himself have not changed. He is most pleased when He can bless us and His work is done through us.

Many people are too passive and fatalistic when it comes to God. "He knows where I live." "If He wants to tell me something, He will." "God already knows what I'll do". We forget to reconcile our "let God do it" attitude with verses like "the kingdom of heaven suffers violence and the violent take it by force", Matthew 11:12. Paul describes the believer as a soldier going to war. Jesus came down to the planet to show us how to "fight the good fight of faith." He is the Captain of the Host of Heaven and will reward those who overcome the enemy.   Overcoming requires a contest; it implies "fighting the good fight of faith," I Timothy 6:12, whether it is in an Olympic arena, or on the back side of the Mountain of Despair.

Being in submission to God's will means I have applied His promises by faith, to my condition.   When I am in alignment with God's Word, I am in His will. God's Word is His will. If God's Word is His will, then we must take responsibility for the choices we make to be in or out of His will. Those choices reflect our obedience to believe and demonstrate a living faith in him.

ABOUT SUFFERING

God does not get glory when His children are in bondage and oppressed, but His Word must stand true even when it must stand alone. He cannot bless disobedience. We need to look honestly at our lives, and determine which things are happening to us as a result of our disobedience and sort them, as best as we can, from those things that God has allowed in our lives to perfect us. Difficulty comes to the saint and the sinner alike. Bad things do happen to good people. Good things happen to bad people. God does not get joy over His children hurting unnecessarily, any more than a good parent enjoys seeing their child in pain. There are times when we allow our children to suffer at the hand of a dentist, or a doctor, but only because we love them and believe it is in their best interests to suffer the temporary pain. God allows suffering for the express purpose of blessing us and training us in the ways of righteousness. He knows that the benefit will outweigh the pain.

In spite of the fact that suffering is many times God's prescription for the advancement of His kingdom and the development of maturity in His children, not all suffering is God's will. To assume that is to passively accept things the devil might want to do to send our way. Some people are fatalistic. They believe that whatever happens is God's will, and they just have to accept it. We know that everything that happens is not God's perfect will. If it were, then why would He inspire intercessors to pray that things be changed. Why would He have tolerated Abraham's reasoning to spare Sodom for ten righteous men? Some people rationalize that they are suffering for Jesus, when actually they are suffering for their own foolishness and unbelief. This is not to say that there is not such a thing as suffering for righteousness sake, or persecuted for the Gospel of Christ. Even Christ learned obedience through the things He suffered. The important thing to sort out is to let patience and suffering do their work of perfecting in us.

Not understanding God's purposes for our suffering leads us to conclude, like the heathen, that God needs to be appeased because He is angry or out of sorts. They believe it must be God's will, when actually, that kind of reasoning only makes God out to be cruel and arbitrary. It makes His mercy fickle and His goodness unpredictable. Jesus said, "No longer do I call you servants, for a servant does not know what his master is doing, but I have called you friends, for all things that I heard from My Father I have made known to you," John 15:14. God wants us to know what He is doing. He invites us to participate in what He is doing and even limits Himself to give us an opportunity to help Him. We may not always understand why He is doing what He does, but He wants us to discern His purposes and work within His Will.

I grew up believing suffering was a virtue and penance a way to get to heaven. With that kind of teaching, torment from the devil can easily be misunderstood as suffering sent by God to mortify the flesh. We must be careful that the cross we carry is not one of our own making. Our flesh is inclined to try and make itself acceptable to a holy God, by taking on punishments and torments not called for by the Spirit of God. It is essential that the believer clearly discern the origin and purpose of the difficulty happening in their life. This does not diminish God's ability "to work all things together for our good," Romans 8:28, but, if it is God, then let His will be done, and bring forth His work in our life. If it is not God, then let us resist the thief, and take back that which he had stolen from us.

Once we have discerned the source of the affliction, we need to ask, "Is God getting glory from my life through it?" Does God look good when His kids get beaten up and robbed by the devil? Or is it our disobedience that has opened the door for the enemy to come in and ransack the temple? Have we tied God's hands in bestowing genuine blessings in our lives because we have believed lies about God? Have we disobeyed His will or opened ourselves up to the torments of the enemy because we have held on to our sin, or failed to confess the sins of our generations past?

ABOUT YOUR SEXUALITY

Our identity is built upon our sexuality. The enemy knows if he can strike a blow here, it can be most deadly.

If he can pervert our identity at its most basic level, he can assault the very core and foundation of who we are. Our male and femaleness, in combination with our spirituality defines the very essence of who we are as a person. Our sexuality and our spirituality form the growth center of our being. Together, they form the nucleus of life that generates the growth and energy needed to build and replenish the individual life internally and to develop it externally. If that growth center is damaged, it affects the growth and development of every other area because its essence permeates every dimension and level of any individual.

Everything we are is based on how we are identified sexually. Our basic identity, dispositions, roles, and biochemistry are all fashioned in harmony and on the basis of being male or female. The devil knows damaging the core of life has far reaching effects. The devastation accomplished at this level is equivalent to sticking an ice pick into the growth center of a kernel of corn. The virility to germinate will either be destroyed or severely hampered, making the kernel essentially dead. Just as the kernel is vulnerable to the outside attack, so is the victim of sexual abuse. The enemy strikes a deadly blow at their most vulnerable and unprotected part. They are struck in the heart. When the ice pick of incest or sexual abuse is plunged into a child's life core, it is no wonder the shame of its violation spills out into their sense of worth and spirituality. The wounds of sexual abuse and incest form deep painful wounds on the soul. The scars and damage can go on for the duration of that life with repercussions even descending beyond it to the generations as yet unborn. Thus, Satan moves, through the sin of the father into the life of his child, and from the life of the child into the lives of their children, moving from son to grandson, to great grandson, even to the third and fourth generations.

Out of the sexual abuses committed against us

comes a strong response to declare our sexual freedoms. Many who proclaim their rights to sexual freedom and declare their gender choice are only advertising their wounds of sexual abuse. They are enraged at the sexual boundaries the Lord established at creation because their own sexual boundaries were disregarded. They rebel against the sacredness of the sexual distinctions between men and women because their own sacredness was violated through abuse. They are steeped in condemnation and guilt because their sexual purity was stolen from them. They chose to forfeit God's will accepting instead the shame and personal rejection of self that accompanies the violation of innocence. They struggle to find a way to deal with the personal conflict within and conclude that the way to regain their freedom is to break God's appointment over them. Homosexuality is an angry protest against their own sexual violation and is motivated from deep, but often unidentified, loss. What appears to be pride and defiance is often a conflicted call for help.

This is especially the case in sexual addiction and pornography. One young man was determined to prove his manhood by "scoring" with as many young women as he could. He had been sexually abused by a female in his childhood and was trying to outrun feelings of homosexuality and impotence. The more he tried to prove his point, the more he became hooked into the control of lust and perversion.

Our body was created to be the temple of God, a temple created without hands, a Holy Place where we could enjoy fellowship with God. God intended it to be a place where our values are crafted and human life is reproduced. In the days of the priests, to violate the Holy Place brought death. From within our temple comes our self-concept. To rebel against, or violate our own, or someone else's sexuality sets in motion a destructive force that eats away in silence, until our life is destroyed.

Have our misconceptions caused disobedience to open the door for the enemy to come in and ransack the temple? Have we tied God's hands from bestowing genuine blessings in our lives because of the lies we believe? Because our sexuality represents a place of intimate communion, it is a place of vulnerability reserved only for God and our spouse. The enemy's early entrance there gives him a great advantage. His deadly blow strikes at our personhood before we are even old enough to identify ourselves as a person. His attack sets in motion a lifetime of destruction. Because sexual abuse opens one of the largest and most devastating doors for the devil's assault on a human life, healing from sexual abuse is essential to freedom and life in Christ.

ABOUT YOURSELF

Many people stumble up against self-acceptance and fall. Some think it vanity to approve of and love themselves, not recalling our Lord's own words that I must love my neighbor as myself. If loving one another is a command and its exercise a fruit of our profession of faith in Jesus Christ, then to love and accept myself is essential to being alive in Christ. I am God's idea. He thought me up before I ever knew I was. Rejecting myself and refusing to accept who I am denies the goodness and love of God creating a deep emotional wound in my soul and a wide opening for evil. To believe humility is insignificance and self-hatred is deception. The truth is, I am truly humble when I accept myself. Rejecting myself and God's love for me is a clever illusion on the devil's part. By disagreeing with God's idea, we automatically agree with the devil's. Whether we sign our lives over to the enemy in ignorance or in full awareness, agreeing with him gives him the freedom to bring any amount of death and destruction into our lives. As long as we continue to consent with the devil, buying into his lies and denying our divine destiny and godly heritage, he will continue to work.

Self-rejection opens the door to self-hatred. Self-hatred is instigated and perpetuated by an evil spirit who specializes in human destruction through accusation and condemnation. When we speak negatively over ourselves, or believe lies about ourselves, we refuse to accept ourselves as God created us. Paul talks about the unobvious sin of self-rejection in Romans 9:20, NIV. "But who are you, O man, to talk back to God? Shall what is formed say to him who formed it, 'Why did you make me like this?' Does not the Potter have the right to make out of the same lump of clay some pottery for noble purposes and some for common use?"

When we disagree with God, we agree with the devil. When we reject ourselves, we write a blank check, 'Pay to the Order of Hatred." We give the spirit of self-hatred and destruction an opportunity to write any amount of evil into our lives they desire. We can be sure the devil will take that to the bank and drain our account if we let him. He may start in the soul, but he never stops there. After he destroys our mental and emotional stability, he goes to our relationships and eventually begins attacking our body. Much of the pain and physical disease we experience is not caused by the aging process, but by the enemy of our soul. He sets up mutiny within our members with the next logical step in the process being to turn us against ourselves.

Self-mutilation is an obvious symptom of self-hatred. Often drawing blood through cutting is perceived to bring relief. One woman would regularly cut on herself and had multiple scars on her arms and wrists. She believed the pain of the cutting to be a relief from the pain of the condemnation, which told her she deserved to die. The reprieve was short lived, however, and each episode was becoming more serious. Eventually the activity resulted in attempted suicide. In her delusion, she believed death would solve her problems with living. She was choosing a permanent solution to a temporary problem.

Once the Devil has convinced us we do not like ourselves, creating resistance and discord among the white blood cells and antibodies is easy. Our autoimmune system is our first line of defense against the invasion of bacteria and disease. Self-hatred allows the enemy to take out that protection and turn the white blood cells against the very tissue they were called to protect. The physical systems designed to guard and heal us begin to devour us. Their assignments to repair and restore are reversed by the lies we believe about the goodness of life. It only makes sense. If I hate myself, is it hard to believe that the members of my body would not follow suit?

Any doctor would describe the most persistent and difficult medical conditions, those in which the auto-immune systems are not functioning, or where the body's cells are not recognizing and accepting healthy tissue as AIDS. AIDS is a good example of this kind of tissue breakdown. To anesthetize us as he caps off his work of destruction, the devil offers us escape-coping solutions like drugs, relationships, sex, toys, and power to temporarily ease the pain. These solutions are laced with the venom of compromise, comfort and death. We drink deeply of the devil's potions and never wake to wonder why we are still dying.

ABOUT THE OPINIONS OF OTHERS

Part of hating ourselves comes from the things we've heard others say about us. Understanding the incredible number of things we may have misperceived as children, it is not hard to imagine what a mess we could have made in deciphering our identity out of the information we've gathered. To complicate the mix, much if not most of what we have come to believe and accept

56

about ourselves is formed from the opinions of others. If we are fortunate enough to receive their blessing in a consistent manner, we come to believe we are blessed. If we are an object of their love and support, we have confidence, and believe we are lovable. But if we grew up a lily among ditch weeds or, an eagle in a turkey pen, we might never discover the truth about who we are. God's Word provides a blueprint, a guiding structure upon which to build a healthy self-concept. Unfortunately, our concept of the Word of God is often that it is an irrelevant, unreasonable, set of pious expectations and commands issued from the courts of heaven by an Ancient, out-of-touch, disinterested and disgusted God. If we refuse to accept the truth of God's Word, we have no reference point outside of ourselves to determine the accuracy of who we are.

The first question of beliefs becomes a question of submission. If I choose to remain willfully unconvinced or ignorant, I will be afraid and divided. Jesus said a double-minded man is unstable in all his ways. As I submit to the Word of God, I apply His promises, in faith, to my condition. Freedom requires bold surrender, not to the evil done against us, but to the truth of God's Word. God's Word is His will, and He does nothing contrary to it. I need to come into alignment with God's Word in order to experience God's freedom. Once my beliefs come into alignment with the truth, I can discern the source of the affliction, and ask God for help.

BULLDOG FAITH

The sad thing about being human is recognizing the incredible ignorance that marks our natural condition. Once we think we have figured something out, we hold on to our opinions like a bulldog. We can as easily accommodate to and adapt to the lies of the Evil One as we can the truth. Once we think we know something, we resist changing our minds because we are afraid it will disturb our equilibrium. We learn to cope and get comfortable, even in the most disgusting situations. The capacity to adjust to our environment is a survival move and not always good for the soul. The ability to fit square pegs into round holes is the human art of denial perfected. "I don't have a problem." "I'm fine."

If we have errors in the hard drive, we will have errors in the print out. It does not matter how carefully I plug in the information, or how hard I try to not make a mistake, if I must access that erroneous information to solve my problem, I will have mistakes in the print out. The mistake has already been made. So much of the task of adulthood revolves around undoing and rethinking the beliefs of childhood, putting round pegs back into round holes. Inner healing begins by simply addressing the lie-based living and behavior patterns that have sprung from the things we have come to believe. God wants to unite our heart and create truth in our inward parts, Psalms 51:5. He wants to bring those defiled and broken parts into healing and wholeness, into their divinely intended function.

Healing is truth-based living in response to the Word of God. Believing the truth and letting go of the lie, no matter how familiar or well rehearsed it has become in our minds, brings freedom. Satan's strategy is to keep us from discovering and desiring the truth. He desires to keep us locked in the prisons of fear and weakness built and held in place by that which is not true.

One young man was split between believing he should live and believing he was not meant to be. The spirit of confusion had so gripped his mind that the most natural thing for him to do was sabotage his own life. As a result of his doublemindedness, he was an easy target for death and destruction. The enemy had gotten in to assault his life with numerous threats and had often attempted to kill him through accidents. As is typically the case with someone who does not value his or her own existence, there is a pull between life and death, light and darkness, goodness and evil. Any such openings present the enemy with ample opportunity to sow discord and defeat in that life. The difficult thing is that many times these beliefs are so buried within us, hidden in lost memories, and the subconscious that only Jesus knows where they are. The key to recovery in any illness is to cleanse the wounded, infected area of the germs and reestablish the body's health. Truth is the only antidote for the lie, no matter where it is hidden or how deeply it is buried.

CHAPTER FOUR

SATAN'S STRATEGY

THE WORLD WE CAN'T SEE

To move with confidence in the battlefield, we must understand more fully the nature and organization of the spiritual world. As surely as we observe the intricate connections and inter-relationships in the physical tangible world of food chains, earth's rotation and satellite Internet links, similar connections exist in the spiritual world. The systems that govern life on earth, function in a myriad of detail from molecular structure and neurotransmitters, to the giant layers of government and concrete arteries that connect this country's roadways from coast to coast of these networks function in valid and purposeful relationships. No less is true of the intricate structure, networking and purpose in the spiritual world. Highly organized and far beyond our comprehension, the spiritual world is far more developed then the physical tangible world of the senses. The spiritual world operates in an unseen hierarchy of governments, powers and principalities, Ephesians 6:12. We are not as aware of it simply because we are preoccupied with temporal things, and because spiritual things are known and revealed to us only by the Spirit not always visible to the naked eye.

ORDERED CHAOS

The first and most obvious evidence of the reality and nature of the spiritual battle that rages in and around us are its casualties. Many Christians are stalled out and stuck. They do not experience the freedom God wants them to have. They can barely get out of bed, much less raise someone from the dead.

They live anything but abundant lives. Their Promised Land is abandoned and overgrown. They are barricaded by Satan like a city under siege. They are casualties that fall, bleeding and dying at our feet. Lives slip through our fingertips. How often do we see a believer start out, eager to follow Christ, only to gradually or suddenly lose out or draw back and grow cold? How often have we gotten to a certain point in our own Christian walk only to fall again into an old habit or pattern of apathy?

To experience freedom and change in our lives, we must first understand what causes our bondage. The mystery that surrounds our questions is no puzzle to God. He is sovereign. In the midst of apparent chaos, God operates in His omnipotent authority, to create an orderly and reasonable arrangement of the events in our lives. He has established certain parameters in His Word and confines the exercise of His will to work within those restrictions. His Word forms the rules and requirements for everything from receiving salvation to the restoration of a godly heritage. That is as true for the universe as it is for the heart.

TIED TO THE SHORE

Many believers struggle, like a boat launched into the river. They are caught up momentarily and carried out into the current only to be jerked back by the rope that is still tied to the shore. We paddle for a while, but we are only treading water. Our vessel is held fast by some unseen cords that prevent us from moving down the river of life. Something holds us back. Fear and failure controls us. We come to a dead stop in Romans chapter seven and can't seem to find our way into chapter eight. If it happened to Paul, what are the chances it would be different for us?

"For what I am doing, I do not understand. For what I will to do, that I do not practice; but what I hate, that I do. But now, it is no longer I who do it, but sin that dwells in me." Romans 7:17. He goes on "For the good that I will to do, I do not do, but the evil I will not to do, that I practice," Romans 7:15. Is he blaming the devil or refusing to acknowledge his own responsibility or is he simply identifying reality?

In other more familiar words, "I'm stuck!" "I'm trapped in this behavior." "I've been to treatment 13 times and still drink." "I can't quit smoking, no matter how hard I try." Paul goes on, "Now then if I do what I will not to do, it is no longer I who do it, but sin that <u>dwells in me</u>." In Romans 7:21 he says, "I find than a law, that evil <u>is present with me</u>, the one who wills to do good."

What does he mean, "sin that dwells in me?" Confusion and doubt set us up to become the devil's playground. I thought I was saved. How can I still be doing this lying, drinking, etc.? Why do I still feel this hatred in my heart? What's going on? Christians don't do stuff like that. We are not experiencing the power of the Cross or the victory it brings and concludes nothing has changed and our salvation is not real.

Many believers are taught to believe that the sinner's prayer is a magical moment that instantly transforms their Cinderella life into "happily ever after." Cinderella's "happily ever after" is not to be confused with the Abundant Life that Christ wants for us. But we forget that because sin was the ruling force in our lives before Christ, it still tries to operate, even in believers, after they have come to Him. Ignorance and disobedience to God's Word allows Satan to continue to build and work in the strongholds he has built in us, even after we are saved. He implements his program of death and destruction even in the presence of Christ, perpetuating his lies and bondage for as long as he can. If he had the gall to come before God and bring accusation concerning Job, what would make him be any more timid in his accusation of us? Though what he is doing becomes illegal once we are saved, and by definition, he is a trespasser, he will do whatever he can continue to get by with as he pursues our defeat. This is war!

GETTING SAVED AND THE QUICK FIX

Many people are told getting "saved" will solve all, or at least a great majority of their problems. Salvation is taunted as the cure all for life's ailments. Coming to Jesus in not a quick fix or a great "natural" spiritual "high". Problems and pain do not automatically melt out of our lives like a bad dream or a nightmare when Christ comes in. "All who live godly in Christ Jesus will suffer persecution," II Timothy 3:12. Persecution is a big part of the perfection and purification process called sanctification. Christians who come into this new life thinking salvation solves every problem would be like one who calls birth the solution to life. Birth begins life. Life has it's own journey. Without birth life is not possible. Just as birth gives opportunity for the life which follows, salvation is birth into God's family and gives opportunity to live in Christ.

New life in Christ is a declaration of war! As we kneel at the cross to acknowledge our sin, we declare war against the old life and the kingdom of darkness. The journey to wellness and blessing begins with new birth. New birth begins at the cross. The Cross is the instrument of death God uses to separate us from the mastery of Satan and our old nature, with its bondages and deceptions. Many people misjudge salvation as the last step to freedom and make it the destination. The power to conquer sin and death starts with being born again. Only when we can cry "Abba Father" through the new birth, are we eligible for a life in the new inheritance and its intended fullness of blessing.

IS THE DEVIL REAL?

Many Christians have problems with believing that the devil exists and that he is an enemy. They fail to comprehend that he still goes prowling about in the 21st century like a "roaring lion, seeking whom he may devour," I Peter 5:8. They confine his history and existence to the Medieval times or the Dark Ages. We attribute our present troublesome conditions to a lack of education, high taxes or the "church". Few would think themselves so provincial and backward as to believe in a real devil who still moves about over the face of the earth, working his fiendish plan for destruction and domination of the human race. Some may be excused for such ignorance because they are uninformed or untaught as to the real purpose and nature of life on the planet. But for those who have been schooled in the things of God, those who call themselves Christians, the question must be asked, "If Satan was in the garden of Gethsemane, tempted Jesus in the wilderness, cast out of Mary Magdalene, and incited Judas to betray the Lord; but is no longer here, where did he go? How was he destroyed? Was he evicted from the planet? Has he gone into retirement? But, if he hasn't gone, and didn't die, and doesn't get old, the question remains. Where is he? It seems reasonable to conclude without a great stretch of faith, that he is still here. If he hasn't left, though he would like us to believe that he has, then people who still talk about the devil causing problems, may not be as unstable or superstitious as we might want to think.

NO TAILS, PLEASE

The devil's disappearing act, unfortunately, is a very effective strategy. If we don't believe we are living in a war zone, will we take the precautions of one who knows the enemy lurks close by? Paranoia is not a greater evil than willful ignorance, nor is ignorance bliss. Believers are not called to be paranoid or ignorant. God has given us power and authority over the devil. "He gave them power over unclean spirits, to cast them out and to heal all kinds of sickness and all kinds of disease," Matthew 10: 1.

"Behold, I give you the authority to trample on serpents and scorpions, and over all the power of the enemy and nothing shall by any means hurt you." Luke 10:19. If the devil can deceive us into thinking he doesn't exist or isn't very dangerous any more, we will not be as apt to stand up and resist him, or put him in his place. Accepting the devil's strategy to convince us he doesn't exist is as deadly as playing softball in a minefield or jump rope with a rattlesnake.

When Satan comes to deceive he doesn't wear his tail and horns and say, "Here I am, come to deceive and destroy you." He dresses in our clothes, wears our perfume, and talks in familiar words of the first person. He doesn't say, "Why don't you have a cigarette?" but rather, "I need a cigarette." Using the first person method of persuasion is his most effective and often used method of suggestion. He catches the unsuspecting with a first person pronoun "I". He convinces us we are hearing ourselves think. We hear his suggestions as us talking to ourselves and buy into the idea. We have made a choice without stopping to think about the choice we have decided to make. His walking among us to destroy us is effective because we are making a deadly assumption that he does not exist.

ERRORS IN THE HARD DRIVE

In other cases, the problem rests not so much in unbelief as in ignorance. The true nature and cause of dissatisfaction with the Christian life, and the experience of continued oppression, is more likely to be one of ignorance and error then deliberate sin. If there is an error in the hard drive of our computer, it does not matter how carefully we input data, there will always be an error in the printout. If our belief system has errors in it, it does not matter how good our intentions, there will always be errors in the behavior. The behavior will be wrong. If your hard drive is programmed to believe 2 plus 2 is 8, you will never be able to successfully balance your check book or reconcile your bank statement no matter how hard you try. Romans 12:1 and 2 tells us to re-program the hard drive by renewing the mind. We are told to rewrite the software using the Word of God for a standard and reference. That means rethinking our belief system and removing all the lies, deceptions, denial, and mind sets we have falsely concluded to be the truth.

A GOD UNTO MYSELF

Another corollary to the devil being harmless is the idea that the devil is helpful. In the last days he will come selling the old product wrapped in new packaging. The devil as my helper is as appealing as ever to the human beings' inclinations to vanity and self-exaltation. Western culture is especially prone to the theory that each of us are a "god" unto ourselves and deserves the worship and acclaim of his or her fellow creatures. The disease of "selfness" sets us up to become the center of our own little world. We practice idolatry by worshipping ourselves. Pride and rebellion make us easy targets for hell's salesman. Whether he convinces us to worship our bodies and boast of our beauty and flaunt our achievements, or to despise ourselves as inferior and pick ourselves apart for our failures, we are, all the same, focusing on the "self". Self is the center of our overabundant attention, service and worship. Satan, seeing our distress, and aware of our desires, and being the "nice guy" he is, offers to help us set up a kingdom unto ourselves.

Who is foolish enough to believe the full body cardboard cut out of Mickey Mouse with my face poked through the hole at the top, makes me Mickey Mouse. The devil is more than willing to sell you a cardboard cut out of whatever it is your heart desires. But remember, all things will be tested with God's refining fire in the Judgment, and

I am sure cardboard is in the same category as wood, hay, and stubble.

The Anti-Christ will not only come selling a false peace, but a fake kingdom where each of us can be a god-king unto ourselves. We desire to set ourselves up as the god of our world and he is here to make it happen. Self-deception and rebellion are fertile ground for Satan. He can walk about freely on the soil of such a one's soul because the ground in that heart is unclean. The blood of the Lamb can only cleanse and protect that which is dedicated to the Lord and set apart for His use. Satan cannot stand on or dwell in, or touch, holy ground. All areas of the life that have not been submitted to Jesus Christ as Lord and surrendered to His will are still fair and comfortable ground for the devil to claim. All who are foolish hearted, arrogant or deceived are open territory and easy targets. The uncovered and unholy ground provides all the invitation the enemy needs to come in. He sets up his strongholds under the pretense of helping us establish a kingdom of our own. Our souls become infested with evil and we are held as Prisoners of War, (POW's), in our own hearts.

A DECLARATION OF WAR

Before we run to the battle, let us first describe the parameters of the war, its stakes, the enemy and the prize. Let us know our authority, our weapons and our Captain. Jesus describes His kingdom within us as invisible. That means the battle in us is also unseen. The parameters of that war stretch from the innermost recesses of the heart to the outer extensions of our expressions. The stakes are eternal, encompassing life and death. We are not the enemy. The enemy is not we, but one of his most effective strategies is to keep us confused on this matter. If he can make us think we are the enemy, he can convince us to turn our weapons upon ourselves. Shooting ourselves is not the our weapons upon ourselves. Shooting ourselves is not the answer, and yet Satan tries to convince us that if we kill ourselves, the evil will be destroyed. He has convinced us that we are the evil we fight. If we believe him, suicide and self-destruction make perfect sense. If he can convince us the only way to eradicate the evil in us is to destroy ourselves, his work is easily done.

Only when we begin to separate ourselves out of this illusion and discern the lie about the enmeshment of our identity with the evil one, can we see clearly to fight him as the real enemy he is. As long as we are confused we are not certain. "A double-minded man is unstable in all his ways," James 1:8. If the first lines of defense are taken out and we cannot effectively separate ourselves from the enemy, there is nothing left to hold him back or stop his full destruction.

I AM NOT THE ENEMY

In order to have a victory, we must have a contest. To have a contest, we must have two sides. As elementary as that may sound, many people have trouble dealing with the trouble in their lives because they do not separate themselves out from the devil. They acknowledge good and evil, but they do not picture themselves on the side of good. Paul said "those things I hate, I do," Romans 7:16. Just because I do them, doesn't mean I approve of them. Nor are doing, and wanting to do what is right, the same thing. Wanting to do good and finding myself continually falling back into evil and wicked behaviors does not mean I am evil or that I approve of evil. It only proves God is right and I cannot free myself.

Many people hate the sin they are in. They have been lied to and taken prisoner, trapped in enemy territory. Being held in a conquered land does not make you a willing citizen of that country. The truth is, as long as our heart struggles against the evil we find ourselves doing, we cigarette. We are held captive by the craving for nicotine, smoking even while we hate it.

WHO IS THE ENEMY HERE?

The first condition for victory and the first revelation we need is to see ourselves as separate from the sin we hate. Paul talks about the "evil" present within him that creates the conflict. What is that evil and the force behind it? Could that evil force be described as a person with a plan; a diabolical personality that schemes against us with his evil agenda? Satan holds a contract out on our life. He wants us dysfunctional and dead. If he can't stop us from getting saved, Plan A, he wants to make us so insecure and ineffective that we are almost useless to God, Plan B. God wants us to overcome and conquer, Plan C; the only acceptable plan for the Christian.

God will not make us do anything without our consent. He respects the free will he has given us. The devil cannot make us do anything without our consent. If he could have, he would have done it already and we would be dead and in hell. Separating ourselves allows us to realize our options. We always have choices. Separating ourselves from the enemy allows us to make a decision, a freedom the enemy cannot deny us. Making a stand against the devil starts with realizing we need to, and that we can. Too often, we let the devil push us around and rip us off while we sit there and let him. Does it bring glory to God, our Sovereign Lord, to whimper and worry and complain about how bad the devil is? Is he mistreating us, or is God training us? "If we faint in the day of adversity," God says, "our strength is small." Proverbs 24: 10. The battle begins when we rise up to fight and its purpose is to grow up in Christ.

MY OWN WORST ENEMY

One of the enemy's first tactics is to trick us into believing we are the evil we hate. Romans 7 is written as an explanation to believers about what was going on spiritually inside them. Before we can understand how entangled we have become with the kingdom of darkness and its lies, we must see our way clear to separate ourselves from them. One of Satan's most effective strategies is to make us believe we have no other enemy than ourselves. If I believe "I am my own worst enemy," I will always be fighting myself. If he cannot get me to agree with him that I am my own worst enemy, then he would lead me to believe I am almost good enough without Christ. The devil does not care what the lie is we believe, because he knows the power of the lie is innate to the lie.

Either he tosses us around with thoughts of never being good enough or almost good enough without God. He chides us for failing to meet everybody else's expectations or exalts us as the answer to everyone's need. We become righteous in our own eyes or too bad to be saved. We have lost our balance. Either our self-absorbed lifestyles and our self-righteousness preoccupations have blinded us from our true need, or our self-hatred is killing us even as we struggle to live. The truth of God's Word sheds light into the darkened soul of both the self-sufficient and the defeated man.

Self-absorption is fertile ground for the enemy. He moves freely through the flesh fields sowing lies, seeds that spring up into bondage. Whether he accomplishes his task by condemning or exalting is of little matter to the devil. He will use whatever works. If he can keep a person bound and defeated by heaping accusation upon them, that is what he will do. If it works better for him to flatter the individual and buy them out with the comforts of carefree living, then that is what he will do. The devil is very pragmatic in his methods, but uncompromising in his intention. To think that we can deal with the devil or stop him, or even detect his activity in our life, apart from God's Word is the height of arrogance and stupidity. Such a one comes close to capturing the essential characteristics of what the Bible describes as a fool.

It is essential that I separate myself from the "sin that dwells in me" Romans 7:17, before I can begin to fight it. Like Paul, we must identify sin as the evil present in me, not as "me". The enemy has been prowling around in our lives for too long. He has masqueraded as "me" and gone unnoticed. We have spent countless hours in self-examination failing to realize the enemy's presence. When he goaded us with our shortcomings and told us we would never change, we never challenged him. He's kept us busy chasing our tails doing his dirty work for him. All he had to do was push the "self-destruction" button and we drove ourselves crazy. The more we listened to him, the worse we got. How many words of unbelief and death have either been spoken over us by others or ourselves, either in ignorance or deliberately? He watched us drive ourselves in circles, castigating ourselves for our failures or lauding ourselves for our achievements. The devil does not care what the lie is we believe because he knows the power of the lie is innate to the lie.

Victory over the enemy calls for separation. Separation from the enemy calls us to walk in the truth. We must proceed against him according to God's Word and not our own. Only His light can make manifest the hidden works of darkness, and loose us from the lies that are causing us failure and pain. As we recognize and acknowledge the truth, we begin to understand Satan's strategy. We are the ones being invaded. We are at war with Satan.

NOT EVERY THOUGHT YOU THINK YOU THOUGHT, YOU THOUGHT

Treachery and lies are Satan's first attempt to break into our lives. Peter Piper may have thought he picked a peck of pickled peppers, but not every thought you think you thought, are thoughts you thought. Many of the ideas, impressions, and even conclusions we think we draw as our own, are merely Satan's ingenious impersonations of our thoughts. They are drawn from deep within the inner workings of the heart where the enemy holds us captive with his lies.

The devil is like a Pied Piper who plays his spellbinding tune through our minds. His mesmerizing sounds do not come like the hissing of a snake, or the roaring of a lion. He sounds like us. He imitates the sounds we ourselves make. He moves along the congested thoroughfares of the mind, slipping in and out of our thoughts as we direct and decide.

He is subtle. Instead of him tempting us with a "you should", or "you deserve", or "why don't you?", he starts the sentence with "I". The devil understands grammar. He knows we usually think our thoughts in the first person; "I" think, "I" want, "I" will. Because we assume that every thought that comes passing through our mind using "I" in its presentation is from me, we rarely question it. Thoughts that come into my mind masquerading as my own are accepted without discussion. "I want him.", "I can drink just this one.", and "I won't get caught." Why would I question what I already hear myself saying to me about what I want? It is a done deal. I buy into a lie and never even suspect I just bought a bag of garbage.

This works especially well if he is pushing me to make a quick decision. "I need a cigarette." does not come up for discussion. I do not stop and ask myself, "But if I want a cigarette, then why am I wearing a nicotine patch?" If I want to quit, why am I stepping out into the freezing cold to smoke this cancer stick? Why do I give the clerk twenty dollars of my hard-earned cash for a carton of cigarettes when my baby needs milk and mittens?" It does not make sense that I should undermine my own self by making a decision contrary to my intentions. Impulsivity pushes us to make decisions contrary to our own survival and well being. This kind of behavior only makes sense when I attribute the thought behind it to the work of an imposter. My battle with the enemy begins with identifying him as he works in my mind.

The deceiver is slick. He knows the only way to infiltrate my thinking process is to trick me into falling for his suggestions. He knows the only way he can get to us begins with the mind. He must get my mind to agree with him before he can go to work in my life and claim me for his own.

If he cannot deceive me in first person pronoun statements, he may try mixing truth with error or omission, as he did when tempting Jesus in the wilderness. If we do not know the Spirit of the Word, he can make error sound like smooth sounding doctrine. "Don't praise the Lord if you don't feel like it, you wouldn't want to be a hypocrite, would you?" Sounds good, doesn't it? I fell for it myself until I read in God's Word, that we are to "offer the sacrifice of praise," Hebrews 13:15. Knowing the Word is essential in defeating Satan as Jesus so clearly demonstrated when He said, "it is written," Matthew 4: 4,7 & 10.

For some, the difficulty comes in sorting out the voices. Again, it is impossible to separate the devil's statements and the chatter of voices if we do not know what the Word of God says. Hearing voices does not mean we are crazy. It means we are hearing voices! They are the voice of the enemy as he battles the mind for control. When I hear voices, that means there is somebody else in the house besides me. These voices are hearable and they are real. These voices may be those of demons, or they may be those of the human fragments, parts of us the mind has created to deal with the task of living life on the outside when the inside system is broken and shut down. We will discuss more of this in the section on human parts, later in this chapter.

We know God created us as a temple for Himself and wants us to walk in His love, power and a sound mind. There is genuine hope and healing for people who hear "voices. Satan can be defeated, and rather easily, once we recognize it is he behind the things we are hearing. He is bound when we bind him, for Jesus said, "whatever you bind on earth will be bound in heaven, and whatever you loose on earth will be loosed in heaven," Matthew 18:18. Binding is a simple fact and a useful weapon, and it works if we believe it.

SEPARATING MYSELF FROM MY ENEMY

The Bible says to take captive every thought, including fear, and make them obedient to Christ, II Corinthians 10:5. We must engage in diligent thought management. Thoughts must be checked at the door of our mental establishment to determine their true identity and origin. They may be an imposter posing as a good idea, or they could be the real thing. The Holy Spirit is faithful to lead us into all truth, if we will be led.

The battle is not won with self-talk or positive mental attitude or self-improvement or penance. We can work the self-effort, self-help methods making resolutions and diets, "white knuckling it" until we are "blue in the face," only to crumble into exhaustion, (the primary cause of depression). The battle for freedom is won with the Word of God. Too many of us continue to "play the tapes" and listen to the liar long after the party is over. The mental bondage the enemy has inflicted upon us remains until we call on the Lord Jesus Christ as truth and light to expose the evil.

THE HEAD AND THE HEART

The head is not the only place lies can be told. As a matter of fact, many times the head and the heart do not believe the same thing. The head can tell you what makes sense, but the heart is hooked in feelings. That is why just telling yourself the truth does not work, and insight therapy can give only a partial answer. Partial solutions to mental and emotional dilemma frustrate the person and deteriorate into more coping and exhaustion. The head knows what the Bible says, but the heart believes the experience. Experiences are easily manipulated especially in a child's mind, where first and often lasting conclusions are formed. We can know about something with our head, but we know it in our heart. We can know about Jesus Christ in our heads, but it is our heart that must experience His love.

The difference between what the head knows and the heart believes is the battlefield. The difference of opinion brings conflict and division in our soul, the seat of our mind, will, and emotions. Our will is caught in the middle, between the mind and the emotions. The will hesitates, drawing tentative and double-minded conclusions. The enemy takes advantage of this hesitation. He plants his lie in the middle of the breach, forcing the separation to become even wider. As the lie grows, the conflict between what the head believes and what the heart knows broadens. This makes it hard to walk in the truth because the double-minded man or woman is never sure where to stand.

Jesus said a house divided against itself cannot stand. How is that any different from a man divided against himself? That person will spend their life fighting themselves. They turn in on themselves, destroying the autoimmune system of their soul, becoming a spiritual AIDS victim. Calling myself the enemy is as profitable as healing myself with a shotgun. Those foolish enough to aim their weapon at themselves are in danger of shooting themselves in the foot, at best, or killing themselves, at worst. Our death is always on Satan's agenda.

HUMPTY DUMPTY AND THE HUMAN PARTS

The only thing that will help us is truth in the inward parts. Psalms 51:6 says, "Behold, You desire truth in the inward parts, And in the hidden part You will make me to know wisdom." An earthen vessel broken into fragments holds no water and is soon dust scattered to the wind. When "Humpty Dumpty" sat on a wall, "Humpty Dumpty" had a great fall. All the king's horses and all the king's men, couldn't put Humpty back together again." Many of us have fallen off the wall. The trauma of falling off the wall opens the door for the enemy to move in and set up lies in the memory.

Children are especially fragile and often targeted. They interpret events as best they can, but often incorrectly. The devil takes advantage of their young and undeveloped minds to cause them to believe things that are not real or true. Because the crisis demands immediate action, a decision must be made. Trauma for a child is having to make a decision without the comfort and protection of an adult. Sometimes the danger is coming to them from the hand of the very ones they are looking to for protection. When the decision cannot be deferred to an adult, the child must make his or her own choice. Because it is difficult for the child to distinguish between fantasy and reality, the enemy is able to set up the lie, or threaten them with further pain if they do not cooperate. He programs them either deliberately as in ritualistic abuse, or conventionally, as in common tragedies, with a system of destruction and error. It is like planting a virus in your software. The program is now contaminated and will not function as it was designed. Their soft little minds are implanted with fear, confusion and pain. These errors become the filters, the experiences through which they conduct future reasoning and development.

DISASSOCIATION

God has given our mind the incredible ability to protect itself from complete shutdown during crisis. The mind has a back-up system running at all times that will take us into automatic pilot when the circumstances become unbearable for the conscious mind. That ability to separate from the present moment is called disassociation.

Do you ever remember staring out the window at school? You were playing marbles on the sidewalk while the teacher was putting the formula on the board. She called on you and you didn't have a clue as to how to answer the question. Your mind had disconnected from its stream of consciousness and the short-term memory was busy playing marbles. The phenomenon is called disassociation. We do it in the dentist's office when we are lying back in the chair. We imagine we are playing volleyball on the white sands of some tropical beach that looks like the picture pasted on the ceiling above the dentist's chair even while the drill whizzes on our teeth.

Not all disassociation is bad, or unhealthy, or has emotional consequences that can destroy us. It is purposeful mental distraction and is useful. Daydream is a mild form of disassociation. All of us have done it. The lecturer is boring and we space out, the sermon is long and we are home fixing dinner or hooking up the boat. We are jolted back into the present reality by our name being called, or by the preacher saying, "Let us all rise", but we have no understanding or remembrance of what was just done. We do not have conscious access to the information and cannot explain the meaning of the word or the function of the formula written on the board. There has been a break in the recording function of our short-term memory.

Disassociation is on a continuum with daydreaming on the one end and soul traveling on the other. The enemy sets up or takes advantage of crisis situations knowing our minds will disassociate. Gaps in the memory are not always just the result of not paying attention. Sometimes not being able to remember is a deliberate effort of the mind to protect the person experiencing the trauma. The mind uses disassociation to separate itself from intense pain and torture by refocusing and distracting itself. During a crisis, the mind "goes away" and separates itself from the event. The mind disengages from the stimuli at hand and searches for an escape. Satan, in his attempt to divide us takes advantage of the momentary mental breakdown and steps into the opportunity to plant a lie. He drives a wedge of fear into the breach using threats and pressure. "It was your fault your parents divorce. You are bad. You are gay. Somebody's going to get hurt if you tell. You are the reason your mommy was always mad. They gave up on you, and if your parents give up, what hope is there for you?"

Under pressure, especially if the child in crisis is unsupported by nurturing caregivers, the child accepts the lie as true. The mind allows that lie to become part of the information system. If that information is in too great a conflict with other information the mind believes to be true, the mind creates a new compartment for the lie-truth. The mind designates a part of itself to keep the disassociated memory away from its stream of consciousness. Fragmentation is the result. In the Humpty Dumpty analogy we could say, a little piece is broken off and left behind to deal with the shame or fear, or abuse, or keep the secret. Through the power of the lie, that little piece is brought into captivity by spirits of fear or shame, etc. Other demons bring other lies and wrap themselves around the little human fragment, building it into a stronghold.

THE TEA CUP AND THE HAMMER

Like Humpty, children shatter. The result is similar to what happens to a teacup when it is hit with a hammer. Their lives are hit with the trauma of dysfunction, abuse, crisis and misunderstandings. The trauma can be something as obvious as physical torture and sexual abuse, or as subtle as being teased by classmates or neglect.

When the teacup shatters, the enemy moves in quickly to take advantage of the piece separated from the core. He wraps it with lies and surrounds it with evil caretakers and spirits of darkness appropriate to the purposes of destruction. Jude 19 makes reference to mockers, in the last days, "sensual persons who would cause divisions." The Greek word for "divisions" means, "to tear off pieces." These pieces of the human psyche are the fragments, the nucleus around which the enemy forms the stronghold. The "little human part" is held hostage by the demonic spirits that surround it. Pain, fear and continued threats, all held in place by lies, prevent the mind from escaping the shrouds of darkness in which it has been wrapped. Many of those parts have learned the only way to survive is to "cooperate" with the enemy.

DIVIDE AND FRAGMENT

Satan's divide and conquer strategy undermines the unity and strength of the person and sets them up for destruction. In sexual abuse, for example, the mind often separates itself from the event by dissociation. A fragment is left behind, to carry the painful memory or conceal the shame. That part becomes hidden and functions only under extreme situations. It is denied access to the conscious, functioning part of the mind and is isolated. The fragmented part often expresses itself through body memories, which come out as emotional or somatic pain that defies medical diagnosis.

Sexual abuse can also cause the mind to create a part that inhibits emotion. The job of this part is to freeze the emotions so the person cannot feel pain or enjoy forbidden pleasure, to protect the person from the danger of emotional involvement and the risks of intimacy. The lie they believe is that feeling causes pain or shame, and to not be hurt again they must stop feeling. As a result, the pleasure center is shut down and emotions are blocked. The person becomes frigid and cold and unable to experience trust or intimacy. Subsequently, their relationships are unfulfilling and their lives lack passion and purpose. They are vulnerable to rejection, depression, extramarital affairs and every kind of mental and emotional dysfunction.

MULTIPLE PERSONALITIES

When the mind's gatekeeper, the will, flees, traumatization and the resultant fragmentation and demonization occur. The Bible describes the invader as a strongman who rushes in past our volition, to set up control, see Luke 11:18-22. He secures the area in and around the piece that has been separated from the whole, and establishes a stronghold or prison within the person. If the mind sometimes allows these fragments to form separate identities, these little human parts take on the task of containing the crisis or conflict so the rest of the body can live. These fragments are in essence the same as the person and contain the characteristic elements of the core person's traits. If these fragments form a strong disposition and continue to function after the crisis is past, the result can be what we call Dissociative Identity Disorder (DID.) Multiple personality or DID manifestations are fragments that have become more well developed and function more externally. Although all human parts have specific jobs assigned to them by the mind, their primary function is to protect the individual. They are the "little human parts" that function under the power of the lie, though many of them are not easily identified and not aware that they believe lies. Though dissociation and fragmentation are mental devises used to deal with difficult and conflicting information, if left to function on a permanent basis, they weaken the mind. The devil uses this strategy as an opportunity to further confuse and scatter the mind, and establish other demonic strongholds within the individual.

Though multiple personalities are a perceived perception and there is, and always will be, only one person in each person, fragmentation and dissociation are the mind's way of coping with difficult or confusion realities. By relegating events, information, and secrets, etc., into the care and keeping of certain designated, mind-created "parts", the mind thinks it can control the damage those events have created. Even though multiple personalities are a "figment of the persons perception" so to speak, to restore the person we must work within the perceived realities of their mind. To bring them to wholeness requires the lies-truths believed by the parts be brought to the surface. Only truth can set us free. Thus, truth must be brought to the "inward parts," just as David cries in Psalm 51. Restoration means bringing the truth to these parts who are confused by the lies and held as prisoners of war within the demonic strongholds erected in the mind and heart of the person. Once they accept the truth, inner healing is easy. Inner healing is simply Jesus reuniting the parts, reintegrating them back into the whole of what He is doing in the person's life. Many multiple personalities have been brought back together into wholeness and unity when Jesus brings truth to the inward parts.

One believer came in with an anxiety problem. She was overweight and used food as a comfort in times of chaos and confusion. As we began to seek the Lord, He revealed a memory that would seem incredible insignificant to the natural mind. She had come from an alcoholic family. Chaos and crisis always followed her parent's drinking binges. One night they came home and set the children in disarray by loosing the cows from the barn. The children were forced from their beds in the middle of the night to round up the animals. As this girl was leaving the house, she grabbed a banana lying on the cupboard. There was never much food in the house, and this looked like lunch, or a safeguard should lunch not be available the next day. Once her mind grasped the lie that food could bring safety, the fragmented and traumatized child subconsciously began to reach for food whenever a crisis erupted.

PRISONERS OF WAR IN OUR OWN SOULS

Most often, the "little human part" takes on a role and responsibility of protecting the core person from pain and danger. They take on the role of a "protectors", and believe they are shielding the person from more pain. Demons offer their help to these "protectors" and promise to empower them, offering help and suggestions for keeping the self safe. Yielding to demons for power and protection makes the little human parts slave to the very ones they've trusted to protect them. These parts believe lies and often perform specific demonic assignments they feel obligated to carry out, even though these activities are contrary and detrimental to the core person's well being. The fragmented part becomes locked in, held hostage by the demonic spirits that perpetuate the lie. Fragmentation is Satan's divide and conquer strategy that undermines the unity and strength of the person. It sets them up for destruction and makes them a prisoner of war in their own souls.

THE MASQUERADE PARTY

To add to the confusion, demons sometimes masquerade as human parts themselves and the human parts sometimes believe they are demons. Because the human parts take their jobs and burdens very seriously, they often carry their resistance and disillusionment about God to great lengths. They truly believe they are "protecting" the person from further pain, not ever suspecting they are part of the devil's plan to destroy the person. As long as they cling to the lies, they are breeding grounds for more oppression and open doorways for the conduction of demonic activity in and around them. This is one of Satan's most effective devices for contaminating the bride of Christ and dividing the Body.

THE FLESH AND THE DOUBLEMINDED MAN

The little human parts are held in the strongholds of Satan. The strongholds are located in the flesh, that unregenerated place in our lives that still needs to come into alignment with what God is doing in our spirits. We call that coming into agreement with God's Spirit sanctification. Jesus called that alignment, conversion. Paul refers to the unregenerated, unsanctified areas of our life as the carnal man or the flesh. Jesus said to Peter, when you are converted, strengthen your brethren. This unconverted, "flip side" contains all the strongholds, doubt, broken parts, double-minded resistance, and hidden resentment toward God. In Romans 7: 15-21, Paul describes the struggle between the spiritman who lives in the Spirit, and the carnalman who does what he wills not to do, as the battle for holiness.

KINGDOMS AT WAR

The war between God and the devil is not limited or confined to the second heaven. The battle is real and it is waged on earth in the hearts of man. The bullets are invisible. They maim, kill and destroy. The alarming number of spiritual casualties will continue to grow if we do not respond to the warning. We need to know and live as people at war. We must dress for battle, and put on the armor of Ephesians 6. We would not think of spreading out our picnic lunch on the front lines or flying a kite in the battle zone, and yet we fail to wonder at the spiritual casualties of those who are falling all around us.

Denying the existence of something be it ever so undesirable, does not make it go away. We are called to the truth. It's time to recognize the enemy, and learn how to use our weapons. The Bible says we "wrestle not against flesh and blood," Ephesians 6:12. Soldiers in war are not "sort of soldiers". They are lean, mean fighting machines, obsessed with a strategic objective and disciplined to reach the goal. They operate under orders and a plan for victory. We are called to be soldiers of the cross in the army of Jesus Christ.

CHAPTER FIVE

THE POSSESSION – (THY KINGDOM COME)

ONLY TWO KINGDOMS

There are only two kingdoms in the world of eternity, and until Christ comes back to sort them out, they co-mingle, existing side by side. God dwells in Heaven. Satan and his kingdom will someday take up permanent residence in the Lake of Fire. You and I do not have a kingdom. Even if I seek to live my life privately, to please myself only, and deny allegiance to any other king or kingdom, I will live in one of the two eternally established residences. There, I will spend my time without end, in either God's Heaven or Satan's Hell. To believe or think I am sufficient in my own self and exempt from God's requirements, doesn't make it true. My beliefs do not define God's reality or dictate His parameters. What I think may or may not be the truth. On earth I am free to live the lies I choose to believe, but the reality of eternity will be a different matter. There I will not be able to change the facts by the way I declare them to be.

TRASHING GOD'S ROOM

The devil hates God. His one desire is to destroy us and make God watch. But he is no dummy. He knows he cannot hurt God by storming heaven or trashing the throne room, so he must settle for the next best thing. All he can do, and do he does, is wreck God's favorite creation, His precious children. This is more easily accomplished, since Satan already roams the earth as the self-proclaimed prince of it.

The war between God and Satan is waged on the human soil of the heart and determined on the basis of human decisions. God will not interfere with His own decree - we are created as free moral agents. Our freedom to choose whom we will worship is the sovereign right of every human creature. Just as God gave Adam and Eve dominion over the garden, He gives us the right to rule our individual lives through our choices.

Satan is not so respectful of our rights and would hang us on a technicality if he could. He started with Adam. Once he had established himself as the lord of Adam, he stripped Adam of every legal right he had. Peter reminds us of the power of agreement when he says, "for by whom a person is overcome, by him also he is brought into bondage." II Peter 2:19. The enemy moved in to claim, without embarrassment or restraint, all of Adam's stuff, including his posterity. Adam's sin opened up the lives of every human being who would ever live, to the curse of demonic domination. Though God does not declare the condition to be irreversible, we were all born into this world under the dominion of an oppressor who shows no restraint in taxing his subjects to death. He doesn't care that people are destroyed. The whole point of his existence is our death. To see us unproductive and destroyed and separated from God is his sweet revenge and great delight.

THY KINGDOM COME

God is secure in His heaven, but His kingdom extends far beyond the "sides of the North", Psalms 48:2. Jesus said it reached all the way down into the very hearts of men. The kingdom is within you, He said. If that is true, then each person is part of Christ's eternal inheritance. If the kingdom of my heart is part of His kingdom and rightfully included in it, then my correct position would be an appointment under His Lordship.

We pray "Thy Kingdom Come, Thy Will be Done". Kingdom management is directly connected with kingdom control. You and I are the prize, up for "grabs" so to speak. We will eventually come under the ownership of God or

Satan, depending, not on them, but upon us. God "won't" make you do anything. The devil "can't" make you do anything, because if he could, he already would have, and our fate would have been sealed in his awful will.

In keeping with the honor of His name, God declares that the sovereign will of man remain present to the end of our choosing time. "It ain't over till it's over." Even the man with a legion of demons was able to press out of his own volition, a cry for help. "But when he saw Jesus from afar, he ran and worshipped Him," Mark 5: 6. The thief on the cross used his last minute option to change his mind and repent, shattering all past records of wrong. Repentance brought salvation to his soul because truth was born in his heart. The freedom of choice remains ours to the end. If God's kingdom is to come in us, God's will must first be done in us. That is why repentance is essential to salvation. Repentance means, to turn around or change your mind on the way you see things, and line up your beliefs with God's. We are all born facing the direction of Hell. To get to Heaven we must stop and turn around.

The kingdom of any king is established by obedience to the will of the king. God has limited Himself to act within the confines of our obedience, regardless of how much He knows, or would like to do for us. If God's foreknowing precluded or negated our free will, God would exist in contradiction to Himself. Jesus said "a house divided against itself will not stand.", Matthew 12:25. The Godhead acting in opposition to itself would destroy the oneness and integrity of itself. God cannot deny Himself or oppose Himself. The kingdom is His, the choices are ours. God never "sends" anyone to hell. Through our choices we have "marked the ballot." God votes for us, the devil votes against us. We cast the determining ballot, voting to accept or reject God's provision and promises to us. Through those choices, we obtain an eternal home.

Obedience is a key to everything in the spiritual

world.   When all is said and done, we really have no power, except the power to choose.   We may usurp temporary control to take that choice from others, but ultimately we will come under the authority of God or Satan.

Jesus said the kingdom of God is within our hearts. If the kingdom over which these two powers fight is within us, then it would be logical to assume the war is within us also.   Much of the battle takes place in the soul, the life control center, made up of the mind, will and emotions. This is the process center where decisions are made.

Temptations are choice options, opportunities, rationalizations, and reasoning Satan presents for us to consider.   If we follow his recommendation, we sin. Sinning makes us his servant and we forfeit our freedom in that area.   God does not desire us to experience constant uncertainty and turmoil from the enemy.   He wants us to live in a secure kingdom that is at peace within its borders.

OUR TRUE IDENTITY AND FUNCTION

We are called and created to be the temple of God, filled with God.   The function of a temple is to provide a dwelling place for a god.   Satan's goal is to indwell human temples, exalting himself as god and king over us.   As he works to establish himself, he vandalizes and defames our character, thoughts and intentions.   He trashes the place, binds the person living there. He breaks our fragile hopes and dreams, scribbling profanity on the walls of our minds. There seems to be no end to what he'll do to try to destroy a human life.   His intention is always the same; to separate us from God and deface the image of God stamped within us. His revenge is insatiable.   To ultimately destroy life is the only thing that he sees as profitable.   If we buy into Satan's lies and accept his reflection of us as true, we will never see the beauty of the Lord reflected in our lives, or accomplish those things that would bring glory to God.

BOUGHT WITH A PRICE - I Corinthians 6:20

The Bible says we are to avoid fellowship with darkness because our bodies are the temple of the Holy Spirit, "Who is in you, whom you have from God, and you are not your own?" I Corinthians 6:19. He goes on to say we are "bought at a price; therefore glorify God in your body and in your spirit, which are God's," I Corinthians 6:20. We are not our own. We are His. We've been bought with a price. God owns us. On all three counts of ownership, God has established legal proof that we belong to Him. We are His because He created us. Anything, great or small, that you make is yours. You have invested yourself in it. Our creations become an expression of who we are, an extension of us. Secondly, we belong to God because He bought us. He paid the price to redeem us by His blood. He paid the price to purchase us back from slavery. He bought us off the devil's auction block and released us to live as free men and friends. The third way we belong to God comes through us gifting ourselves back to him. If someone gives you a gift, it becomes yours. We have "given our life to Jesus," making Him the official legal owner and rightful resident of our lives.

I am called to be the dwelling place for the Spirit of God. A temple without a deity is like any other building. We only serve our full function as a temple, we only take on meaning and purpose in our life, when Christ Jesus comes to dwell in us. His presence is life. Paul knew the secret when he declared, "to live is Christ." We serve the dual function of becoming a dwelling place for the Spirit of God. We are built as "lively stones" set together to form a larger, living organism called the Body, the arms and feet and heart, of Jesus Christ.

If we are going to accept the call and function as a dwelling place for God, we are going to have to relinquish any other notions of who we are that might contradict that pronouncement. Many times, the thing that most interferes with God's mighty working in us, is our own concepts of who we are. Statements like, "Oh I couldn't do that.", "That's not me.", or "I am German." excuse us from allowing the Holy Spirit to change us. Change is as essential to the transformation process as life is to development. Without transformation, God cannot develop His full purpose and change in our lives.

DUAL OCCUPATION

So how can God and the devil be in the temple at the same time? How did Goliath continue to live in the Promised Land? Why are the tares allowed to grow along side the wheat? Is it any wonder that the soul becomes a battlefield for the wrestling out of all temptation?

Life in God is not meant to be a matter of compromise, or peaceful co-existence with the devil. God is giving us the opportunity to use the authority He has placed inside of us by the abiding presence of the Holy Spirit. For us, it is a matter of believing in the authority and power of the stronger man who has come to tear down the prison walls in our lives and set us free. Goliath lived in the Promised Land, trampling and plucking out of it what he desired, until God came against him in the form of a boy, David. Our weakness and disadvantage is nothing for God. He is able to achieve the destruction of our enemy if we are willing to pick up the five smooth stones and stand up against the strongman in the name of our God. It is a matter of choosing to submit to God and resist the devil. Change comes when we let the Holy Spirit have the control He needs to accomplish it. Our part is a small, but essential part.

It is like the little hinge upon which the great door is hung. Though it is small, it is not insignificant and though it is not large, it determines the amount of freedom and usefulness of the door. Just as the hinge can hinder the function of the door, we can hinder the intentions of Jesus Christ and His purposes for our life by our stubborn resistance or unwillingness to move. Just as it sometimes takes oil to loosen up the hinge, it takes the oil of the Spirit to loosen us to function freely.

ARE YOU DONE YET?

Some still think that, given a little more time, education or advantage, they can master their own life and destiny. Others just want to get rid of theirs. The question the Holy Spirit asks each of us when He begins dealing with our souls is, "Are you done yet?" Are you done trying to make something happen on your own? Aren't you tired of trying to make your life do what you want? Isn't it time to give it to Jesus and see what He'll make of it?

To some, it seems to be a hard decision. They cannot see what advantage giving their life over to God would accomplish, because they still have not seen what disadvantage being a slave boy for the devil has been. They are under the impression they own the house they live in and are their own boss, lord of their own private dwelling. If that is the case, we seem to have overlooked a minor detail of ownership. If you are the landlord, when was the last time you collected rent from the devil, and how long are you going to let him stay camped in your life without paying taxes? If the devil does not pay his rent, and he does not own the property, then he does not have any business being there. Evict him. Serve him his walking papers. Take him to court. Don't be shy or apologetic. He's the one who owes you an apology for defiling you.

RETAKING THE TERRITORY

God's command to Joshua was to take back the Promised Land. Every place Joshua set his foot, the Lord promised to be with him. But that was then, this is now, we reason. Then, under the leadership of Joshua, a new generation of brave warriors came to take back the land of their rightful inheritance. Now, we see a new generation of warriors coming in to take back the land for their king. The story of the natural history of Israel accurately parallels the spiritual condition found in the lives of many of the redeemed today. Our lives, like the land, have suffered from years of neglect and abuse under the devil's oppression. Years of carelessness "complacency" and the absence of spiritual vitality, have allowed the enemy to gain footholds he should never have had.

Our reasoning and mental assent have been perverted and twisted. We no longer see spiritual truths clearly or hold them as relevant to our condition. Satan has set up strongholds of fear and footholds of doubt. The abundant life Jesus talked about in John 10:10 is not a part of our experience. Many of us feel condemned and defeated, struggling for years trying to overcome things that should have been gone a long time ago. We are afraid to ask for prayer, afraid to admit our lives are tangled with cords of iniquity. We wrestle with giants, and are locked in strongholds of depression and despair. We wander in an unidentified wilderness of fruitlessness. Like the Promised Land overgrown with briers and filled with barricades, our life with God is more a trophy of Satan's conquest then Christ's cross. They have suffered from years of neglect and the absence of spiritual leadership. Their lives bear the marks of the devil's rule. In spite of our profession, the reality of ownership is more often in the one who has control of the property, than in the one who holds the deed to the property.

DID THE DEVIL DIE FOR YOU?

If not, then why do we feel obligated to live by his suggestions? The devil is not a "nice guy". Ever! Nor is he the winner he claims to be. He is a liar and a treacherous foe who has been defeated. His only power is the power we give him in our minds and hearts. Even though he is whipped, he continues to craft his lie and lure the ignorant and unaware into his death pits. As long as we let him run his operations in our soul, he has a right to do so. Satan continues to use whatever he can to achieve his ends, spreading lies and creating illusions of terror in our hearts. His methods are obvious to the Holy Spirit who would warn those who listen to the voice of the Good Shepherd, but difficult to discern for those unaware of the promises and power of God's Word. The devil can promote his subjects or castigate them. He can dance with them, charm them, and promote them to great and enviable heights if it serves his purpose, or he can plague them with difficulty if they resist him. No matter which way he does it, his only purpose it to steal, kill and destroy us.

WAR GAMES

Understanding the enemy's strategy and decoding his plan is essential to winning any war. The devil's strategy is old, but effective: Divide through debate, doubt, confusion and pride, and conquer through isolation, abandonment and fear. The strategy for war looks impenetrable until we start to understand that as impressive as it may look, his hold on the believer is illegal. His claim to the lives of believers will not be upheld by the Universal Code of Justice in the High Court of Heaven. Defeating the devil in court becomes a simple matter of faith and obedience. Claiming our rights as "blood bought property of the Most High God," breaks the enemy's cycle of plundering and pillaging of the enemy in our lives.

That is why winning the war with Satan plays out to look more like a courtroom debate then smoking guns and dropping bombs. Winning the war with Satan is based on truth, not might and power. It is rooted in understanding the enemy's strategy and our authority. Because the outcome has already been determined, and the Lord Jesus Christ has been declared the Victor. Actual combat is really waged more as enforcement and executing the conditions of that victory then battling to conquer. Putting the enemy on the "witness stand," with Jesus being the chief witness against him, opens us up to the truth which sets us free. That is why, "Taking the Devil to Court" is a more appropriate way of fighting spiritual warfare than drawing him onto the battlefield or, demanding he let us alone.

THE CIRCLE OF LIFE & SATAN'S STRATEGY

To understand the devil's attack against us, we can start by drawing a circle. Allow that circle and let it represent everything about your life: your body, soul, and spirit; your mind, will, and emotions; your past, present, and future; your hopes, dreams and talents; your ministry, relationships, finances and generational inheritances. Know that the enemy seeks to establish strongholds of darkness within every area of your life. Many of those strongholds will be patterned after those he has already built in the bloodlines of your past generations. The patterns are often so similar from one generation to the next, that with close observation of the first, we can almost predict the second. The devil is not creative and has no scruples. If it worked once, he'll try it again. The patterns and problems developed in the stronghold resemble those of coming out of the lives of our parents and grandparents. The enemy is familiar with the weak spots in your life and what has worked in the past to shut you down. He will direct his attack into that area.

Molly came in with physical pain and complications from an automobile accident. She was a strong believer and walking in faith. When we reviewed her history we found several other members of her family had been in severe car accidents, including her father and her sister.

The area of her body that had suffered the greatest damage, were similar to problem areas in her father, circulation in her legs and hemorrhaging. We discovered her grandmother had been the victim of several severe car accidents in connection with drinking. Through her drinking, she had opened up the door for the enemy to harass her children in the exact same way he had attacked her. Because of her disobedience and sin, the enemy was able to continue to perpetuate the cycle of destruction in them in the same places he had gotten hold of her.

Patterns of sickness, three or four generations of stomach pain, getting killed in the same places, becoming pregnant at the same age as, are hard to ignore. If the curse without a cause does not come, we would have to call these a coincidence and the universe would be out of control, not a good thing for God or us.

THE STRONGHOLD

Each stronghold begins as a seedbed of iniquity passed down through the generations before us. Their unrighteousness becomes our legacy. The devil sows the old lies into the fresh new soil of the child's innocent mind. As the child grows and begins to make choices, the enemy comes along to persuade that little one to believe those lies. If he succeeds, the child is brought into bondage and the cycle begins again.

THE DEVIL HAS A NAME

The stronghold becomes the base of operations for the strongman. Each stronghold's specific name and character reflects the personality of the head honcho. There can be many demonic spirits in each stronghold, forming a hierarchy of command. They network together to bind the person in their web of evil. When Jesus dealt with demons, He had no qualms about asking the demons their names. Because He never did anything outside of the perfect leading of the Holy Spirit, there must have been a reason He did it and a lesson to learn. Too often, we live in a fog when it comes to dealing with the devil. He does not raise his hand and identify himself willingly. We need to be more specific in dealing with him. The more specifically we can identify him, his name, behavior, or point of entry, the better chance we have of convicting him. The more evidence we have, the stronger we demonstrate our resistance to him and purge ourselves of his presence. A soldier who desires to destroy the enemy does not shoot in the general direction of the enemy. He or she will aim for the whites of their eyes and stand their ground.

SUBDUING THE ENEMY

The strongman can only come in when he overpowers the one who dwells in the house. The strongman tries to infiltrate the person's will often by treachery and guilt, and in some way gain the cooperation of the person. That is how he must come in. The strongman is able to overwhelm the vessel's first and rightful occupant. He may live on the roof or in the cellar at first, but his one desire is to completely take over our lives and disconnect us with our life source. If we let the devil walk on us, he will. If we don't know our rights and authority, he will subdue us with his. The devil has a kingdom and some power. God has allowed the devil some leverage and legal access to this world. Satan uses that opportunity to spread his hateful propaganda and established strongholds and kingdoms in our hearts and affairs. We were once the appointed rulers, but through deceit, Satan subdued us and took over. Satan has gained a legal access to God's creation through the rules of conquering. "To whom you present yourselves slaves to obey, you are that one's slaves whom you obey." Romans 6:16. God is completely in control. He is good and just, but He allows Satan to test the hearts and affections of men to reveal our true heart and intentions. God does not send anyone to hell. He never has. As a matter of fact, everything He has done since the garden was and is to prevent us, warn us and protect us from that most awful of ending. Redemption is God's response to the strongman's destructive intentions and His invitation to us to be saved.

IF NOT THE DEVIL, THEN WHO?

To deny the devil's existence is to give him an unnecessary advantage. If we deny his working among us, we will have to find other explanations for the presence of the evil and injustice at work in us. Taking the devil out of the picture makes it much more difficult to explain the existence of evil, if not impossible, to answer the hard questions about the things we see happening to us and around us. Job, Chapters 1 and 2 would be a good resource for any one who denies the active interference of evil in a pretty good man's life.

If the devil is not among us, then we are forced to conclude that either we ourselves, or God is the origin of temptation. If it be God, He contradicts what He says about Himself, when He reminds us that He "cannot be tempted by evil, nor does He Himself tempt anyone," James 1:13. We do know, however, that God will allow certain things, including temptation, to come into our lives to test us. When we are "drawn away by our own desires and enticed," as James 1:14 describes it, we are being drawn into the front lines.

We know that if we refuse the love of the truth, as Paul warns us in II Thessalonians, that God Himself will send a strong delusion that we should believe a lie. "The coming of the lawless one is according to the working of Satan, with all power, signs, and lying wonders, and with all unrighteous deception among those who perish, because they did not receive the love of the truth, that they might be saved. II Thessalonians 2:10, 11. And for this reason God lie, that they all may be condemned who did not believe the truth but had pleasure in unrighteousness."

ANCESTRAL DEMONS

Recognizing the power and pattern of generational inheritances is not intended to be a glorified excuse for being irresponsible. We are not looking to find justification or blame our parents. We are only trying to obtain an accurate picture of the conditions and weaknesses that plague the soul and body so we can successfully treat the condition. The lives and stories and patterns experienced by the grandparents are extremely helpful in determining the specific areas of weakness we may encounter. The enemy knows exactly where those spots are and directs the majority of his attacks there. Why should he try to enter through a wall when the door is cracked open? The devil is familiar with his new victim because he is familiar with family. In some cases, he's been around so long he could even introduce himself as an "old friend of the family", a familiar spirit, privy to every secret and sin in the family line.

It appears that these evil spirits are often assigned to certain families and given specific assignments over those families. They are known as "familiar spirits" because they are familiar with the family's secrets, sins and debt record of wrongs. They know who's paid up, and who still owes them something. Whom we yield ourselves servant to obey, his servant we become is their legal claim to the life and limb and the property of their victims. Spiritual ownership and property rights are as tangible and true in the unseen world as they are in the natural. As a matter of principle, things are only true in the natural because they are true in the spiritual. The devil is a legalist that demands payment and claims rights to "his" property. If his victim doesn't know his or her rights as a believer, it's all the better for the enemy.

doesn't know his or her rights as a believer, it's all the better for the enemy.

THE RULING ANCESTRAL DEMON, RAD

Even as God has a plan for our life, and watches over us to bring us into that plan, Satan has a plan for us. That plan is called destruction and is watched over by the principle strongman or familiar spirit assigned to our life. The Ruling Ancestral Demon, RAD, is the record keeper. His job and intention is to oversee our personal destruction. He knows the open doors, cords of iniquity, active curses, words and vows against us, who is in the stronghold, and who oversees it. He knows who answers to whom. Binding him and displacing him are an important part of strategy for healing and deliverance. We will discuss more about how to deal with and identify him in the chapter on procedures.

A BEACHHEAD OF RIGHTEOUSNESS

God is not pleased that the place of His glory has been broken into and dishonored. He cannot dwell in a place where evil inclinations and worldly pursuits continue to rule the life. God has much better things in mind for us. He desires to establish His character of righteousness in us and bring us into fruitfulness. He is not glorified when His children are scattered under the evil hand of demonic oppression. God took the initiative to restore us. To repair us, He must redeem us.

Through His Spirit, His love established a beachhead of righteousness in us. In the midst of death and destruction, God comes and plants salvation. Hope begins to wash over the soul, drowning in the unbridled sea of condemnation and sin. God looked past the ruin of our prodigal lives. We had wandered down the streets of frivolous living and been caught in the pens of pride and rebellion. His love looked past the hardened hearts and saw His children lost and homeless. He saw the folly we pursued and the useless attempts we made to refresh ourselves at the poisoned wells of material goods and worldly pleasures. He longed to restore the once glistening fields of grapes and oil, now left smoldering and charred from the effects of the curse. The magnificent man, who had once been given dominion over the earth, and authority to subdue it, was now marred and wasted, like a burnt field of stubble. His only hope was in God's plan.

HELL'S FOR THE DEVIL

Hell was created for the devil and his angels. God never was, and still is not willing that any should perish. So why does He let the devil have such power to deceive and destroy, if He knows what the devil has in mind? God is always fair and just. The devil only has the power we forfeit to him. Power and control and authority remain constant and are ever present in the world. They shape and determine good or evil by the nature and character of the one who wields them. When Satan holds them, the world and its inhabitants suffer. God had given that power and dominion originally to both Adam and Eve. Jesus regained the power, as represented in the "keys of hell and death" when He descended into the lowest parts of the earth, or hell, and took them back. He received that power and re-established God's kingdom rule of righteousness on earth through the church. We are the church through which He declares victory over the "gates of hell". As believers, He gave us power over all the power of the enemy, and promised that nothing would by any means hurt us, Luke 10:19. If He has given us an 18 wheeler to drive over the devil's head, why should we fuss over Satan's go-cart? God wants us to exercise that power through our faith in Him, to reject the devil's lies and break down his strongholds.

over our enemy. God has restricted Himself to working within the perimeter of our obedience. "Son of man, they who inhabit those ruins in the land of Israel are saying, Abraham was only one, and he inherited the land. But we are many; the land has been given to us as a possession. Therefore, say to them, 'Thus says the Lord God: You eat meat with blood, you lift up your eyes toward idols, and shed blood. Should you then possess the land? You rely on your swords, you commit abominations and you defile one another's wives. Should you then possess the land?" Ezekiel 33:23. Obedience to God becomes the key to blessing and abundance and God's fulfillment of His good pleasure in our lives.

OLD TESTAMENT, OBSOLETE?

The Bible is a book of instruction. It is a word to the wise. Whosoever will believe and act upon the words contained there in will be blessed. The Book of God's Word has an Old Testament and a New Testament. We must not assume that the things recorded in the Old Testament are obsolete or unimportant for us. They were types and foreshadowing of the real. Let us not be too quick to throw out the Old Testament, forgetting that the law is fulfilled in love. Love is obedience to the counsels of God. Through love, the law continues to be validated in the dispensation of grace.

How many times have we read through the Bible and skipped over Numbers, Leviticus and Deuteronomy because they were "boring" or had nothing to say to any current situation. We must be careful not to over look the foundation principles of truth as they originated from the mouth of God. Our declaration of the "way things are" does not make them so, true, right, fitting or legal.

Many Christians get stuck in the New Testament, and forget there are valuable lessons in the Old Testament as well. God is the same throughout all generations. His

Word and standards of holiness do not change. Jesus Himself said He did not come to do away with, but fulfill the law. Not one dot or comma will fall to the ground, until all is fulfilled. Jesus' reverence for the Old Testament leads us to examine it more carefully for clues as to our present state of difficulty. As I have searched the scriptures, I have been most encouraged to find that the answers are found in the origins.

CHAPTER SIX
OPEN DOORS AND THE EXISTENCE OF EVIL

SIN OPENS THE DOORS

When Adam sinned, the devil tore the door off the hinges of our lives and came busting in like a roaring lion. When Jesus came, He laid down His life to become a new door. Jesus said, "I am the door," John 10:7. He came to reseal and restore safety and salvation to the inner chamber of our lives. Accepting Jesus gives us access to His life. He becomes the protection and power we need to sustain our life through His grace. One thing we must consider, however, is that as protective as the door may be, it does not shut itself, nor is there any protection unless it is closed. Jesus has made provision for His people, the sheep of His pasture, to be safe and live in the security of His love, but He has left it up to us whether or not we would choose His sheepfold and accept the protection it offers.

Satan gets in through sin. Sin opens doors and creates entry points for the devil to come into our lives. Just like the thief gets in if the doors are left hanging open, Satan takes advantage of the openings in our life. Without Christ we are as vulnerable as a fort with its gates left hanging open. The openings and secret passageways tunneled into and under the blocks and timbers of the city wall, if allowed to remain, provide Satan with the opportunity to lay siege to the city of our soul. We are vulnerable and have become open to his attack any place where we have permitted his lies to remain.

The stability and protection God desires for us is undermined by these gaping wounds and unguarded holes in our lives. The walls are broken down, making us an easy target for invasion. Many of these "weak spots" and doorways were opened through the sins of the generations past. Our parents suffered from the shortcomings and addictions and afflictions of their parents, who, in turn suffered from the offenses and neglect and sins of their parents, and ad infinitum.

THE WORLD, THE FLESH AND THE DEVIL

Sin, separation and offense, comes from one of three general sources, the world, the flesh, and the devil. The world represents all those wounds and offenses done to us or against us by others, whether that be people or systems. The flesh is our natural predisposition to sin. It is tilted in sin's direction, and if it is allowed to choose the direction for our life, it will always choose to lay on the couch and eat potato chips. The devil is the author of temptation and the promoter of discord between God and His creation.

THE DEVIL AS A PSYCHOLOGIST

The devil has been studying people for a long time. He knows us because he knew our parents. As a matter of fact, he knows our parents and our grandparents much more intimately then we ever will. He knows, (knew), their weaknesses and their secret fears, and blackmailed them every chance he got. Through guilt and condemnation, he made many of them slaves to his evil disposition until they became perpetrators of evil themselves. Every time they gave place to the devil, he planted himself more firmly in their lives and took more territory. It began with Adam and Eve. Their cooperation with the devil's suggestion to not believe in the goodness and fairness of God was the sin that gave him the initial right to come in and dominate them.

Sin is surrendering ground to the enemy. Surrendering means giving up or losing control of a position. Each time we sin, we give the devil another place to stake his claim in our life. Unbelief opens the door to disobedience. Disobedience is the sin that surrenders ground to the devil and leaves us unprotected and vulnerable to his theft and destruction in our lives.

SETTLING ACCOUNTS

Many Christians forget the continuity of God as He visits His mercy and judgment from generation to generation. If our generations who have gone before us have given the enemy a place in their lives, he inherits that place in ours, as well. Through the lie he works to carry the momentum of his activity from one generation into the next. Until my family's sin account in the "Heavenly Ledger Book of Justice" is reconciled with the blood of the Lamb, somebody will be held responsible for those sins. The story of the Gibeonites in Joshua, Chapter 9, illustrates the generational principle of transference of the spiritual account from one generation to the next. Joshua and the children of Israel were blitzing through the land of Canaan, taking captive the inhabitants. When the Gibeonites realized the strength of Joshua's army, they devised a plan to save their lives. They tricked Joshua and his men into giving their word to the Gibeonites that they would not destroy them. When Joshua found out the truth several days later, he declared, "This we will do to them: We will let them live, lest wrath be upon us because of the oath which we swore to them." Joshua 9:20. God honored Joshua's promise to spare the Gibeonites, even though Joshua and the rulers of Israel had been deceived into thinking these Hivites were not from the land of Canaan.

Everything went well until Saul came to power, several generations later. He got the bright idea to destroy the Gibeonites, so he did. His successor was King David. During his reign, there had been a mysterious famine that continued year after year, for three years. David sought God and found out why He was angry. And the Lord answered, "It is because of Saul and his blood-thirsty house, because he killed the Gibeonites." 2 Samuel 21:1. King Saul, in killing the Gibeonites, had broken Joshua's word to them. The devil's rampage against the children of

Israel was legal because of the oath that had been made to keep the peace for wrath's sake. When Satan saw a breach in the promise, he took advantage of the opportunity to demand that God bring judgment and wrath upon His people. God knew Satan's demand was legal because the words of the truce had made a provision for judgment if the vow was broken. Only through confession and repentance was David able to settle the account and shut the devil down. Because this was before the cross, grace and forgiveness came through restitution. Restitution and repentance, in this case, required the death of seven of Saul's sons. Until the children of Israel acknowledged their unfaithfulness and sin, the power of the curse was free to devour them.

EATEN UP AND WASTING AWAY

The same principles are true in our lives. Until we break them, negative spiritual influences and generational curses have the power to bring forth trouble in our lives. The simplest way to break them is to obey God. Leviticus 26:39 – 45 clearly says the reason the children of Israel were "wasting away" and being "eaten up" by their enemies was because of "their iniquity ...and also in their fathers' iniquities, which ARE with them they shall waste away. 'But if they confess their iniquity AND the iniquity of their fathers, with their unfaithfulness in which they were unfaithful to Me, and that they also have walked contrary to Me, ... if their uncircumcised hearts are humbled, and they accept their guilt, -- then I will remember my covenant with Jacob, ... I will remember the land, (42) ...for I am the LORD their God."

God does not want us to be helpless victims forever, subject to His wrath or Satan's revenge. We do not have to be subject to the generational sins of our father's past, stuck in an insidious transfer of bondage and death. Jesus Christ brings good news. He has come to break the patterns of destruction through our confessing those behaviors as sin against the holiness of God. Jesus desires to deposit grace in our account. When we acknowledge the sins of our fathers and repent of our participation in those sins, both "knowingly and unknowingly," we silence the devil's argument against us and bring ourselves back under the blessings of those who are under the Lordship of Jesus Christ.

CREATURES OF GRACE AND MERCY

When we confess the sins of our generational bloodline and repent of ours, grace and mercy can be applied to our condition. The Word says we can be new creatures. Old things are passed away, and all things become (begin to be) new. We can clear the record and start clean by claiming our new inheritance. God desires that we exercise the rights and privileges we have as the Redeemed. His promise is good. Faith is believing in something enough to act on it. Our faith takes God's promises to the bank. The demands of sin and death have been satisfied, paid in full, by the death of God's beloved Son.

Since the death of Jesus, the New Testament has been in effect. Hebrews 9:14-17 says that where there is a testament, a will, there must also be the death of the testator. A last will and testament is in force only after a man dies, and "has no power at all", while the person is still alive. Jesus was made the Mediator of the new covenant because His death paid the debt owed under the first covenant, making it possible for "those who are called may receive the promise of the eternal inheritance," Hebrews 9:15. Those who are called are whosoever will, because we know that God is not willing that any should perish, II Peter 3:9.

The Lord's death put His last will and testament into effect. God was able to legally establish His Son's inheritance. It allowed God to rewrite the old will and testament of law and death into the new will and testament of grace and pardon. Grace and pardon do not give us a license to sin, nor is it forced upon us. The New Testament gives us the opportunity to claim a new inheritance of grace and pardon, but just like any last will and testament, the beneficiary is not endowed until they lay claim to their inheritance.

As with any inheritance, the beneficiary is free to choose to treat lightly or even despise the assets and gifts others have gathered for him. Sons of preachers and granddaughters of evangelists can throw away their godly heritage if they so choose. On the other hand, a solitary soul, the orphan and the outcast who has been birthed into no special advantage, can finish first if they obey the Lord. The great and final determination of our inheritance rests in our obedience as it is expressed in our attitude.

GATES, GRANDPARENTS, AND GENERATIONAL SINS

Grandparents are the people whose children grew up and had children. They are the purveyors of the family trust and all that it includes. That family trust or inheritance is that which is passed on from one generation to the next. Because the accounts and accomplishments of each generation are passed down through the bloodlines from one generation into the next, all the good and bad stuff that belongs to them becomes the property of their children. All that they could not take with them is left behind to the next of kin. Their children become stewards of the inheritance for the next generation

THE SINS OF THE GENERATIONS

Just as we are heirs to the material possessions of our parents and are physically a result of the unique combination of genetic material found within their gene pool, we receive and reflect their spiritual legacy as well. That spiritual legacy is a mixture of good and bad traits, tendencies and predispositions. The nature and documentation of the transfer of a spiritual legacy is found scattered throughout the Old and New Testament. The iniquity of the fathers is mentioned in a few other places in addition to Exodus 20:5. Exodus 34:7; Leviticus 26:39; Numbers14:18; 14:33; 16:27; Deuteronomy 5:9; 2 Kings 21:21, 22:13; 2 Chronicles 29:6; 34:21; Ezra 9:7; Nehemiah 9:2; Job 21:19; Psalms 51:5; 109:14; Isaiah 14:21; 65:7; Jeremiah 3:24; 14:20; 16:19; 23:27; 31:29; 32:18; 44:9; Lamentations 2:11; 5:7; Ezekiel.2:3; 18:2; 18:19; Daniel 6:24; 9:16; Hosea 10:9 and Matthew 27:25 all address the issue of generational iniquity, and the pain it causes. To say that this must be an important concept for us to understand, might be an understatement.

CORDS OF INIQUITY

From these scriptures we see that God makes it very clear in the Old Testament, not only that the sins of the former generations will come down into the children's lives, but that the children also carry a responsibility for those sins. In some respects, it is as if they had committed them themselves. Among the many passages that tell us about the sins of the generations is the one the LORD plants in the middle of the Ten Commandments, probably so we would not miss it. There, in Exodus 20:5, He describes Himself as a "jealous God, visiting the iniquity of the fathers on the children to the third and fourth generations of those who hate Me. But showing mercy to thousands, to those who love Me and keep My commandments."

Negative inheritance can govern a myriad of details and cover a vast number of situations. Predisposition to addiction, weakened resistance to sexual perversion, perpetual unbroken patterns of abuse and victimization, propensity to lust, anger passed from father to son, mysterious reoccurrence of accidents or sickness, family histories of cancer, etc., are just a few of the endless number of things shaped and affected by spiritual inheritances. The length of the lives of the grandparents, their occupations, marriages and significant stories passed down not only offer important information about the behavior and spiritual well being of our ancestors, but serve as accurate predictors of our own futures.

If we can decode the mysteries of our family bloodlines and identify the generational patterns, we will be more equipped to understand the present and prepare for the future. We often describe these "patterns" as a coincidence, fate, luck or as accidents. Accidents are not accidents, and there is no such thing as a coincidence. As a matter of fact, the Hebrew language has no word for the English word "coincidence." That should tell us something about the relevance of coincidence as an explanation for the unexplainable things that happen in our lives.

Sometimes uncovering family secrets and finding lost family lines can be a challenge, especially if there has been an adoption. People who have been adopted as children or come from blended and broken families, may have more difficulty in uncovering their background and personal history, but that does not prevent the sins of the fathers from being visited onto the children. The spiritual legacy is a well-established, though often greatly underestimated, fact of Scripture. Our Western mentality and selective hearing in being more preoccupied with our personal rights and equal opportunities for life, liberty and the pursuit of happiness cause us to balk at the thought of spiritual differences. Many people are as oblivious to their spiritual condition as they are to their histories, especially in America. We are so removed from the generations proceeding us that we know very little about their physical lives, let alone their spiritual past. We may be entertained by the interesting oral traditions and treasury of stories handed down to us, never suspecting the rich information they provide. We flirt with the nostalgia of antiques and old heirlooms, but fail to see ourselves as the recent addition to an ongoing collection of ancestral sins and ancient secrets.

SOUR GRAPES

" It is not fair!" Why should we have to suffer for the sins and secrets of our fathers? Ezekiel addresses this protest in his discussion of the old saying that Israel had used to describe the realities of generational transference. No longer would Israel need to use the proverb "the fathers have eaten sour grapes, and the children's teeth are set on edge," because God wanted to establish in them a more firm understanding of personal responsibility for actions. "Behold, all souls are Mine; the soul of the father as well as the soul of the son is mine; the soul who sins shall die. But if a man is just and does what is lawful and right; ...and has withdrawn his hand from iniquity and executed true judgment...walked in My statutes and kept my judgments faithfully - he is just; he shall surely live!" Ezekiel 18:2-9 condensed. We can do something about the generational curse handed down to us by our fathers by choosing to walk uprightly.

Though inheriting curses was not fair, it was legal. Satan won all the prizes when he got Adam. The deal included all Adam's authority, his mandate to administer the business of Eden and his kids. Through Ezekiel, God reminds us of our prerogative and power to chose. He acknowledges the transference of the father's sins visited on to the children to the third and fourth generation, but points to the way out. Ezekiel 18 establishes clearly the facts of personal responsibility while acknowledging the truth of generational transference. Though each one will die or live with the consequences of his own choosing, we cannot live without acknowledging the spiritual disposition within which we must make those choices.

Though Ezekiel God is making it clear that our actions and choices will bring consequences, those outcomes can be different from what our parents experienced. We are not doomed to live with our lips puckered in the acid taste of sour grapes just because our fathers eat them. We have since come to know that nothing can separate us from the love of God which is in Christ Jesus, Romans 8:35. The devil can make no absolute declaration about our salvation. Each one has a free will. He wants us to understand the sour fate of our fathers does not have to trap us into a life of bondage, but that He has made provision for us to secure a life of blessing. The final outcome does not have to be dependent on the choices of those who have gone before us. Satan's hold on people is conditional. If anyone, at any time, should desire to follow after the commandments of the Lord, he is eligible for freedom.

The open doors and advantages the enemy had gotten in our lives are subject to change in accordance to our choices. The old nature is subject to Satan's domination because the old man is servant to Satan. The devil continues to lay claim to his victims through the inheritance laws, but those laws are always subject to the higher law, which declares each man to be a free moral agent and at liberty to choose whatsoever he will. Our new life becomes operational through our choice to serve a new master but doesn't end there. Liberation of the Promised Land was not accomplished by crossing the Jordan or seeing Jericho fall. Cooperation with the work of the Holy Spirit begins with a process of loosing that breaks the hold of the old sin nature and frees us from the default of sin. Just as reclaiming the Promised Land was, so the pursuit of liberty is a fundamental and ongoing part of life.

WHAT ABOUT SALVATION

The transference of the iniquity of the father onto the children cannot prevent us from getting saved. Salvation is an individual transaction between each person and the Lord Jesus Christ. No man will be saved or lost without having his or her own say so in the matter. The sins and generational cords of iniquity, however, have more to do with blocking our blessing and productivity after we're saved, than they do with preventing our salvation, although, obstacles that hinder both our salvation and our sanctification are present in the generational inheritances.

Our choices about the content and condition of our spiritual inheritances have about as much to do with our own choosing as a runner has in selecting his starting position in a race. Both our freedoms and limitations have been affected by our spiritual legacy and only prove the power of sin's effects to be passed down.

Though spiritual inheritances have nothing to do with actually being lost or saved, the predisposition to spiritual weakness and patterns of difficulty begin to map out a life pattern for blessings and curses that need to be addressed. Though we may experience the difficulties of our parents and grandparents, it is not automatically predetermined that we must accept those conditions categorically. Spiritual and genetic inheritances create advantage or disadvantage that have nothing to do with our freedom to run the race. They only speak to the ease or difficulty with which that race is run.

SUM IT UP

Cords of iniquity and unconfessed generational sins continue to provide open doorways for Satan to access the soul of the believer. Those sins, though not necessarily ours, give him access and legal entrance into our lives even as believers. Any thing or place not cleansed by the blood of the Lamb affords a place for the enemy to stand. Coming to Christ and acknowledging the sins of our generations as a strike against God's holiness cleanses the ground and frees us from those ancestral mandates. Once we have fulfilled God's prescriptions to confess the sins of our generations past, the enemy can no longer perpetuate his destructions. The enemy cannot stand on the Holy ground washed by the blood of the Lamb nor can he maintain strongholds in areas that have been redeemed through confession and repentance.

The blood of the Lamb and the cross become the great equalizers in a human life. The authority of the Word of God and salvation through the cross, applied to the condition of a human heart, sets men and women free whatever their condition may be. The advantage of understanding the power of spiritual inheritances comes from the Word but must never become an end in itself. The truth applied with understanding and honesty to the conditions of the heart creates the new advantages and opportunities for the abundant life Jesus promised.

MEDICAL RECORDS

Spiritual inheritances are as true in human experience and disposition as are the physical distinctions captured in the DNA. The spiritual and physical worlds of experience seem to run parallel here as can be seen reflected in the medical field. Taking a medical history is common practice in diagnosing physical ailments. Patients are asked to reflect back similar conditions past or present, in other members of the family. Answering questions regarding the medical history can verify the past presence of certain conditions and helps establish the diagnosis. It does not offer a cure, however.

Though biological inheritances are often seen as rigid and difficult to change, alterations in the spiritual inheritances can be made more easily. The sin cords of iniquity that have tied us to the destruction and death of the past can be broken. We are not predestined and doomed to failure, locked in bondage without remedy. The effects of severing those spiritual ties are real. They can be felt in the spirit and soul of the individual, even to the point of experiencing physical healing in conjunction with the spiritual restoration.

One set of siblings researched their generational tree through relatives and the Internet and found out that they had roots in royal bloodlines. The stomach problems they were experiencing went back four generations to a European grandfather who had had intestinal obstructions and chronic pain. We dealt with their pain as a spiritual attack and unhooked each one from the particular sets of lies that had bound them to the pain. After several sessions, one of them reported marked improvement in her abdominal area and the pain was gone. The second one experienced a decrease in pain levels.

Another woman not only experienced the patterns of physical weakness similar to those of her father and grandfather, but the predisposition to severe car accidents as well. She was in constant pain and had undergone numerous surgeries from an accident she had been in ten years ago. She was continuing to experience complications with the healing of her left leg, the same leg her grandmother was suffering with. Her father had also injured his leg in a car accident. Both the father and woman's grandmother had been in numerous car accidents in their lifetime. Many of them were severe and had to do with drinking. All three experienced complications in clotting and circulation due to the accidents. The enemy had moved his stronghold from one generation into the next using the same method of destruction on both father and daughter. When we prayed against the hold the enemy had gotten through the generational line, she noticed marked improvement of the circulation in her leg and an improvement in its response to therapy almost immediately.

Often when pain is mysterious and unresponsive to medical interventions, it is good to suspect and pursue the possibility of spiritual origin. Symptoms of a delicate stomach and chronic worrier/caretaker are commonly found together. Anger often accompanies arthritis and inflammation. Research has shown a correlation between anger, T-cell levels and cancer. Certain physical and emotional conditions seem to go together, many times with the emotional situation being the primary force that holds the physical conditions in place.

Pain is the physical response to many spiritual maladies. Improvement in our physical condition often occurs when the lie that holds the person in emotional bondage is removed. Sin begins as a thought in the mind and is endorsed by the will. It then works its way like a cancer through the body of its host until it has eaten up both the spiritual and the physical life. It saps the vitality of all layers of our existence, often extending its destruction beyond us, to victimize our as yet unborn or unsuspecting offspring.

The medical field teaches us that many things can be carried and predicted through the blood. Physical ailments, mental illnesses and addictions often begin as diseases of the soul. Their presence can be traced through the generations past and identified as clearly as DNA in the blood or mental imaging in the brain. The soul's diseases are primary. If left unchecked, they can create the chemical patterns of disease and deterioration that destroy the body.

It is time the church recognize the powerful truth God has given us in His Word to explain not only spiritual phenomenon, but gives us the remedy for our physical diseases as well. We can see their interconnection in Jesus' ministry of forgiveness and physical healing to the paralytic carried by his four friends, see Mark 2:1-12. The distinction between whether a person suffers from a demon or a physical condition may ultimately be of little importance, as Jesus is the answer to both. The Scripture uses deliverance and healing interchangeably on occasion, with some references to deliverance being described as healing, and some healings accomplished through deliverance.

Rather than become caught in a conflict of semantics, or feel pressure to become a social services referral agency, the church needs to take responsibility to deal with the whole person. Sectioning people up, referring them to specialists and professionals only fragments and frustrates them and delays healing. Jesus deals with the whole person and seeks the restoration of every part of the life.

GENE POOL OR ENVIRONMENT

Scientists and psychologists have been arguing for decades over the predominant influences that shape our lives. Some thinkers have argued we are a blank slate, a tabla rasa, while others insist we are a product of our environment. Others contend that we are a biological organism, a product of our innate inheritance and the gene pool from which we were generated. Even if the disagreement could be resolved in favor of one over the other, what have we solved? The Bible describes our problem as a combination of innate unrighteousness and a less then ideal environment. Pig farmers have known the truth for centuries. We can take the pig out of the mud pit and groom it for the fair. We can paint its toenails and powder it with talcum, but the minute we let it go back to being a pig, it will go back to rolling in the mud. We can physically get the pig out of the mud, but we can not get the mud mentality out of the pig. Neither a changed environment nor education can convince the pig to choose a more sophisticated way of life.

PERSONAL SIN

In addition to the inherited openings and vulnerabilities passed down through the sins of the generations, we can create doorways and entry points of our own. Many of the predispositions and potential difficulties we face are made worse by our own choices to believe lies and sin. Many of us who have accepted Jesus Christ as our Savior still struggle to experience the life transforming power of the Holy Spirit. We walk in inconsistency and dissatisfaction, even though we try hard to serve God. We make a start for heaven, but seem to still be tied to hell. We get going for God, only to be pulled back into a rut that keeps us in a position of passive unbelief. Can you see patterns of loss or behavior or dysfunction that moves from one generation to the next in your own life? Let us bring it a step closer to home.

What is your family noted for?

Honesty	Jealousy	Generosity
Integrity	Competitive Attitudes	Lying
Mental Instability	Aggression	Yelling
Control/Manipulation	Angry Outbursts	Closeness
Sexual Perversions	Chemical additions	Love of God

What kind of things did your family experience?

Divorce	Abuse	Favor
Abortion	Success	Feuding
Witchcraft	Poverty	EarlyDeath
Christianity	Bad Luck	
Attention Deficit	Recurring Health Problems	
Pregnancy out of Wedlock	Sibling Rivalry	

Do you see the patterns beginning to be repeated in your children? Are the members of your family open and warm, or secretive and cold? What do these things have to do with anything, you might ask? What does favor or an untimely death have to do with spiritual inheritance?

The books of Leviticus and Deuteronomy list many tangible ways in which the devil tries to assail us, collect on the unconfessed sins and operate the curses in our lives. Deuteronomy 27 and 28 describes a long list of specific sins and the resultant curses they bring. The devil tags these offenses like a red herring and uses them to continue to lay claim to us as he opposes and oppresses us in our new creature walk.

The only way to get out from under his accusation and the onslaught of destruction is to answer him with truth and humility. Answering these questions frankly will give us a place to start in tracking down the enemy and locating the openings he is using to get into our lives. We cannot talk the devil into mercy or a moratorium. We cannot reason with him or expect special privileges. The only way we can get free from the devil's hold is to confess and repent of those things he is using to hurt and steal from us. The only thing legally able to remove stains of sin and bondage is the blood of the Lamb of God slain for the sins of the world, blood for blood. Only His blood can destroy the work of the destroying angel in our lives.

DENIAL

Until we know and admit to the presence of the cancerous tumor we will not take the steps necessary and available to remove its deadly presence from our body. The same is true for our spiritual condition. For many Christians taught to accept an over-simplified version of grace and sanctification, do not discern the need to take deliberate action to resist the devil. We think that once we are a Christian, we should not be having any more problems with lust or anger or jealousy. We deny the present condition and reality of our soul and comfort ourselves with the lie as long as possible. The past is the past so let it be the past, we reason. Wishful thinking and denial only give the enemy more time to strengthen the devil's grip on us. We supply the ignorance and he supplies the energy to continue his takeover of the kingdom within us.

If you are still going through Chicago, you are still not out of Chicago. If we continue to suffer from the effects of guilt or be plagued by an urge to drink, or battle the temptation to lust, we are still not free from them. If we are willing to put up with the enemy's activity in our lives, we will have it. If we are content with coping, we will have a hard time embracing the cure. If we do not square off with the enemy and take back that which is ours, he will never give it to us on his own. We let the parameters of our old behavior dictate the size of our cell rather then openly embrace a new life Christ. The doors left open by the last generation are causing us to catch colds living in the draft. Worse yet, the roaring lion who goes about seeking whom he may devour is hungry and on a hunt. How much easier it is for him to walk through an open door then a closed one? Denying we have a problem only keeps the door open and us living at the mercy of the lion.

When he is in control, do we wonder why bad things keep happening to our family and us? A behind-the-scenes look at the life of Job is enough to convince us of the origin of the assault on us, see Job Chapters 1 and 2. The Lord of life has shone His light of truth into our hearts to make manifest the hidden works of darkness. If we choose to disregard His truth, we will be left in the dark. Denying the presence of the problem or allowing it to go on undealt with only causes it to grow bigger and more powerful.

Admitting the truth and stepping out of denial may be embarrassing at the moment, but coming to the light and confessing the true nature of our condition is essential for new life. Just like surgery is, for the moment inconvenient and unpleasant, in the end, it may be the only satisfactory medical solution to the cancerous tumor.

Confessing our faults breaks through the denial. The Bible says, "confess your faults, one to another, and pray for one another, that you may be healed," James 5:16. Confession talks about admitting our sin. Healing may refer to the emotions, the spirit, our relationships, or our body. Healing for any area requires that we deal with our sin. Confession is almost a lost art in the western world. We are taught to stay strong, and never admit it when we are wrong, lest our opponent get an advantage in us. As a result, we carry for years and lifetimes, burdens and pain that could be disposed of in minutes, hours or days if we would have confessed our part in them.

Why would someone suffer all their lifetime with migraine headaches, if the solution might be as simple as confessing the sins and unfaithfulness of the generations past, as prescribed in Leviticus 26:39-40? Why would we choose to live in pain and failure, when living as new creatures in Christ and experiencing the fullness of His peace, was as easy as living in forgiveness and true faith? The suffering that people put up with that they do not have to is incredible. The lost energy and productivity in the kingdom is beyond calculation. We refuse the simple remedy of repentance and obedience and go around looking for something else to relieve our distress. We wander in our error, looking for someone else to blame. We make it God's fault we suffer, or sight our deprived childhood, or a church full of hypocrites as the reason we can't get better or experience the new creature promises of God.

WORDS

"Sticks and stones can break my bones, but words will never hurt me." is another catchy little lie the devil likes to tell. Not only can words hurt me, they are powerful enough to kill me. Through the spoken word, universes were created and life was formed. The Word was all God used to create the worlds and their systems! The Bible says there is "death and life in the power of the tongue," Proverbs 18:21. James warns how "the tongue is a fire, a world of iniquity." James 3:6. Through little words great fires are kindled. Words spoken over us by others are a creative force that either blesses or curses us and yet most of us never give it a thought or ever question how our words might be affecting the receiver. Parents are in an especially influential position when it comes to words because of their relationship with their child. The Bible says words fitly spoken are like apples of gold set in pictures of silver. Words can be as beautiful and up-building as they can be deadly and devastating.

We use words to build sentences and selves. When the powerful people in my life use words that are true to describe me, and they are spoken in love, I grow up, Ephesians 4: 15. When the words spoken over or to me are lies, they cut and bind me. All too often we are unable to discern clearly the true nature of the words spoken to us and our minds find it difficult to interpret the message they bring. Double messages bring confusion and pain. They often couch the truth in such a way that it is hard to know what the person means or what they are trying to say. If we are afraid to speak our mind, or express our feelings outright, we couch them in sarcasm or jesting. We attach disclaimers to our words or tack "I was just kidding!" at the end of serious complaints. Our listener does not know what to believe nor are they able to respond in truth.

Initially as children, because we cannot discern the nature of the words accurately, whether they speak truth or error, we welcome them all into our spirits. We treat them with reverence as legitimate and honor the speaker, usually a parent, like they are a god. We drink them in, never suspecting that we could be drinking poison. The words spoken over us become a part of our soul, spirit and self, as surely as the food we eat assimilates to become part of our tissue. Words spoken over us have the power to become us. They create a framework on which we hang our images, ideas, and personal identity.

Many of our beliefs and concepts are formed during our childhood. The interpretation of childhood experiences forms the basis for the interpretation of subsequent experiences. As adults, we continue to use them to define danger and describe ourselves to others and ourselves. We seem to accept our childhood impressions and beliefs without ever sorting through them later, to determine how accurate and reliable they are. We never get around to separating out those that are true from those that are false. As believers, God's Word commands that we speak "what is good for necessary edification," Ephesians 4:29.

Soon the words spoken over us become the words we speak over ourselves. Our self perceptions, observing and learning about me by watching what I do, is a circular type of learning and prone to keep me stuck in a system of personal error that becomes self-fulfilling prophecy. I have bought into the lies of others, and become confused by their error and deception. If the words spoken over me are positive, they are called a blessing. If the words spoken over me are negative, they become a curse. It does not matter if I speak them or they are spoken by others. The more often I hear them, the more familiar they become. The more familiar they are, the easier it is to believe them.

Words create beliefs and beliefs create actions. I may not have heard the curse spoken more than a couple of times, or it may have been ages ago, but the power they hold over me can be as strong as the day they were first proclaimed. In time, I do the destroyer's work for him by repeating these harsh and condemning words over myself every time I fail, or fall short of the mark. The accuser of the brethren has succeeded in convincing me, through other people's words of my unworthiness, and unlovability. It doesn't take long before I'm rehearsing my own undesirability and have learned to play the "tapes" for myself.

VOWS

If the enemy is not able to wound us through hurt and offense, he has another feature, his "Word Trap and Enslavement Method." If we are wise enough to reject his lies spoken onto and over our lives by others, we may make the mistake of reacting in the opposite direction by making a vow. How may times have we come back with "I'll never treat my kids like that.", "I'll never let another man get close to me, ever", "I'll never let you know how I feel.," "I'll go to my grave hating you.," or "I'll never speak to you again?." We declare things like, "I'll show you.," "I'll get even with you.," or "You think I'm bad now, I'll show you what bad is all about." How many people, in an attempt to make somebody else "pay", end up being the kindling for the fire they hope to burn their enemy with? How many daughters get even with their fathers by becoming promiscuous and pregnant?

One pretty young fourteen-year-old had gotten herself dangerously close to getting killed in a poorly thought out runaway plan. She was angry with her father for trying to tell her what to do and setting a curfew. She and a girlfriend had taken to the streets of a large inner city neighborhood. They were looking for drugs and some fun, but ended up getting raped.

Another way the words are turned on us is self-inflicting condemnation. Words like, "I hate myself., I'm ugly., I'm fat., I'll never amount to anything., I'm stupid.," become deadly weapons in the hand of our enemy. These words become fixed as vows that begin to operate automatically in our lives. These words and vows, whether we know it or not, become silent, but powerful motivators in our lives. Vows are powerful words spoken to counter attack powerful words, but words are words, and words create life or death.

On several occasions, people have come in with severe cases of self-hatred. They admit they had wished they would die and admitted trying to take their lives. "I've wished I could die hundreds of times. Anything would be better then this pain." The more we wish for death, the more we offer ourselves to it. Death can actually begin to claim us through a breakdown of our autoimmune system, opening us up to infections and sicknesses, fatal accidents, or a general devitalization and loss of energy.

Vows are promise words in which a person "binds themselves to an act, service or condition," Webster's Dictionary. Vows are sometimes reckless promises that come out of a crisis. Words and convictions spoken in haste require payment. The world I have just created settles down over my soul and spirit like a silent monster mist that colors it all brown and broken. Ecclesiastes 5:2-5 talks about the seriousness of a vow and the open doors they create that make us debtors. Woe to the one who is a debtor to the devil!

Vows are sometimes spoken in desperation as bargaining efforts to obtain that which we feel is impossible to accomplish on our own. We promise, invoking the power of God or a demon, pledging upon the altar anything necessary to get what we want. We consent to certain and sometimes horrendous stipulations or conditions. Just as genetic coding material dictates the direction of biological life, vows once set in motion begin to unconsciously control and influence the course of our spiritual and emotional life. The outcomes that spring from these vows form predictable patterns and responses.

Vows and promises initiate patterns and requirements from not only the person who made them, but can be required of their generations as well. These patterns can be observed repeating themselves in the family for generations. Vows and curses can also hold the key to the mysterious cycles of destruction, bad luck, accidents and loss that continue to plague certain individuals. Many of these patterns often reoccur at the same ages or approximate times and locations as they did in the generation previous.

VOWS AND UNFORGIVENESS

Vows made in anger or retaliation carry the extra fire of unforgiveness. Anger, retaliation and unforgiveness all make a convenient highway for the devil to ride on into our lives. Because he can only move in areas where sin and uncleanness still remain, unforgiveness is like paving an eight lane super highway for the devil to drive on into our lives. Unconfessed sin is Satan's natural habitat. When we make vows born in hatred and bathed in rage, revenge and jealousy take over. We have just unknowingly opened doors and created a perfect environment for the adversary.

Many times in our vulnerability, we feel the need to protect ourselves. We are tempted to hold on to the anger and unforgiveness like they were our best friends. Words and vows like "I'll never let a man get close to me ever again!" or " I'll never let my parents into my life because they will try to control it!" become commonplace. Our vows to "make them pay" become the prisons we find ourselves locked in. We hide behind the anger and think having a tough intimidating attitude will hold the world at bay. Little do we realize that the very powers we are using to protect us are the prison guards that keep us in the bondages we despise.

FORGIVENESS

Forgiveness is the key to breaking the hold of sin, whether it be the atrocities of abuse committed against us, or the vows we have declared against others. Forgiveness releases us from the judgment we have rendered against others and frees us from the judgment that has come upon us. The law says that we reap what we sow. If we have sown hatred and unforgiveness and judgment and anger into the lives of others, we will reap hatred and unforgiveness and judgment and anger. That is the simplest meaning of "Judge not lest you be judged," Matthew 7:1. Until we forgive, the road is paved with sin. Sin always gives the devil access to us and allows him to exploit our lives.

Breaking a vow is done by reversing the process used to make one. Reversal is a simple, straightforward principal that works because it is based on the law of reciprocity and fairness. The words spoken to break the curse or nullify the vow are just as powerful as those used to make it. We must repent of the sin, withdraw our judgments and let go of the injustice that formed and fueled the vow in the first place. If we feel the injustice is a valid complaint, we can turn our case over to the High Court of the Universe where Jesus Christ sits to judge the living and the dead. We can be sure that no injustice or offense or deliberate wrong will go unpunished or un-righted in His courtroom.

ABUSE AND TRAUMA

Another way the enemy gains entrance into our lives is through abuse and trauma. Great physical or emotional pressures when inflicted on and are absorbed by the human soul, body, or spirit break open gaping holes in the protective walls of our lives. The breaks allow all manner of evil to come flooding in. Many of the decisions made during a crisis or trauma are not based on scripture, but survival. We feel unable to take action. Fear and terror subdue the will and rise up in that moment to capture the heart, with plans to stay a lifetime.

The favorite tactic of the enemy is to raise the question "Where was God?" Somehow, making God look like the bad guy is an effective distraction and smart tactic in calling us away from the truth onto a side road. The lying spirits fill our minds and hearts with questions about the goodness of God, and leave us resentful and bitter, hanging without hope. It works well to get the heat off the devil and focuses doubt on the faithfulness and love of God.

Trauma and tragedy come in many forms. Some of them are naturally occurring, while others are purposefully inflicted. Common trauma may include accidents, death, loss, unexplained disruptions of safety and routine and natural and financial disasters. We call many of these attacks upon our lives "accidents," implying there is no particular cause or reason for their happening. According to Proverbs 26:2, however, something causes everything. When we accept the event and rationalize its presence in our life, not suspecting an enemy has done it, we do not resist him. The devil uses our passive acceptance and our ignorance to enter into the exposed area and establish a lie and set up a stronghold.

Trauma that is inflicted on us deliberately is Satan's concentration camp tactics to break us down. He takes advantage of our weakened condition to impose himself upon us. He perpetuates the damage he's done by lying to us about our innocence or deceiving us about our freedom. He tells some victims it is their fault and others that people owe them. He promotes control and manipulation in some and self-pity in others. Each time we take the devil's advice in responding to the abuse and evil done in and to us, we give the devil more room to work his destruction. Sin and evil, if left unchecked by truth and repentance, snowball into an avalanche that buries us under a ton of pain that may end up taking our lives. Once the enemy is in, he likes to stay. He begins taking up residency in our lives plotting against our innocent, as yet unborn offspring waiting in the next room.

SOUL TIES AND LOYALTY TO DYSFUNCTIONAL RELATIONSHIPS

Soul ties are any ungodly bondage or connection made between two people. God binds us in relationships, but the devil brings us into bondage. Having a soul tie is like having two signatures on the contract. We are not completely free to buy or sell, or transact business without the approval and cooperation of the other person. God wants us free to follow Him, regardless of who in our life might agree or disagree. Soul ties are formed through abuse and violation of God's laws. Any avenue that is unclean and illegal in the sight of God can provide an unholy highway for the enemy to travel on. He rides in on the sin and binds his victim with pain.

Soul ties are held together by demonic control and restrict the freedoms of both people. Even relationships that God intends for us to enjoy can become abusive and unhealthy if sin is present. Parent/child, husband/wife, and sibling bonds can become bondages when abuse, sexual perversion, and cruelty are present.

Soul ties are broken by acknowledging our part of the sin that gives the devil access to them, and releasing the other person from their hold on us through forgiveness. Often I lead the person to verbally "give back to the other party, those parts of themselves they gave to me, and take back to myself those parts of me that were taken by them." I then ask God to "make me one with myself and at peace with Him." After the soul tie is cut, ask the Lord to apply His blood to the wound for quick healing.

THE POWER OF THE CROSS TO CANCEL THE OLD INHERITANCE

We consider ourselves fortunate to inherit a large sum of money, or good looks, or a keen intellect, but we often overlook the importance of the primary inheritance, our spiritual position of blessing. We fail to recognize the power this spiritual legacy has in describing the strengths and vulnerabilities of our starting point and the potential problems we may encounter on the way. We do well to consider the concept of inheritance, being careful not to confuse the idea with the doctrine of predestination or fatalism. We must remember that for the Believer, all things are made equal at the cross of Jesus Christ, including any negative spiritual inheritance, open doors or demonic strongholds. Because of the death of Jesus Christ, the old debt has been satisfied, the accounts have been paid, and whosoever will, can have a new inheritance through new birth in Christ. Only the cross and the power of regeneration can significantly affect and alter the legacy of sin. Just as in the natural, the inheritance is not based on merit, although at times it is adjusted on merit, it comes to us based on our relationship with the benefactor. Spiritual inheritances are not based on God owing us anything, but on our relationship with His Son. A slave or a man who has not come into sonship through adoption into the family of God is left to his own resources. Self-righteous efforts in sanctification will only ultimately wear out anyone trying to make himself better. Our new inheritance in Christ Jesus, however, makes us heirs to the throne and joint heirs with Him in His kingdom to come. It cannot be earned or bought, but must be received freely, in the same spirit in which it was given.

CHAPTER SEVEN

THE PATTERNS AND PREDICTIONS

THE DEFAULT IS THE PATTERN

The physical and spiritual histories of the relatives, especially blood relatives, reveal the nature and value of our inheritance, as well as describe the pattern for our future. The default programmed into the hard drive will be the path chosen by the computer, unless a specific command is made to alter or redirect the task.

Many who have accepted Jesus Christ as their Savior still struggle to experience the abundant, life transforming power of the Holy Spirit. Their walk is inconsistent and unsatisfying even though many try hard to serve God. They make a start for heaven, but seem to still be tied to hell. They get going for God, only to be set back, pulled into a rut of passive unbelief. Others struggle against invisible adversaries and habits, making choices that appear to be deliberate sabotage of their personal walk with Christ. For some, the patterns of loss and dysfunction that move from one generation to the next in a family lie close to the surface and are easily visible. For others, the roots lie buried deep in the secrets of the past, creating struggles that are extreme and devastating.

Many people are stuck in the default mode in their lives. They can quickly identify the things their parents did, vowing they will never do that to their kids, and yet time after time, they find themselves helplessly caught repeating the pattern. Even those who make a conscientious effort to do things differently find the power of the past influencing their behaviors. The pre-programmed predisposition to act a certain way prevails in spite of efforts to change it.

The strength of the pattern can be seen both in its accuracy to predict the future, and in the difficulty one has in breaking it. Often the pre-programming is so powerful and similar to that of the generation that preceded it, that the people of the next generation not only experience things like their parents and grandparents, but tend to experience those things at the same ages and under similar circumstances as their parents. "Like father, like son" is more then a quick explanation of the way things are. It is common to hear a mother complain of her 16 year old daughter getting pregnant, only to find that she was pregnant herself at the same age. Car accidents, cancer, back injuries, broken relationships, divorces, attention deficit disorder, and mental illness, to name a few, all seem to cycle down from one generation into the next.

It is true that all have sinned and come short of the glory of God. Our grandparents were not perfect and our parents seem to have followed in their footsteps. For all the sophistication of modern technology, failure has been part of the pattern since the fall of our first parents in the garden. Sin and the curses are still part of life. The fact that thistles still grow and men still sweat and women still have pain in childbirth are all signs that the curse is yet among us.

The original sin still affects us today, even if we are saved and walking in obedience. Satan is collecting royalties off the first sin, every time someone practices it again. The undeniable facts is that the promise of eternal life exists side by side with the curse. Sin brings bondage, and perpetuates its destruction in death. Eternal life calls us to freedom. We cannot assume things will go forward without conflict until the presence and effect of sin are eradicated from the world. The promise is that the more we comply with the will and Word of God, the better our chances will be of experiencing the blessings of a productive life on the earth in spite of the curse.

The father's sins open the door for the troubles of one generation to come tumbling down into the lives of those in the next. If our parents and grandparents lived godly lives and dealt with the sin in their lives, and destroyed the inroads it had made in their souls, our task will be easier. If they allowed the doors to be opened and did not attend to the business of living holy lives, the lion that feeds in darkness, will continue to stalk through the family rooms of their innocent and even as yet unborn children, devouring them even to the third and fourth generation.

Sin opens the door, repentance closes it. It is important to recognize that specific sins bring specific curses. Even as different violations of the law each have their own consequences, certain maladies are connected with certain sins.

OUR TRANSGRESSION AND CROSSING THE LINE

The law cannot be ignored. Jesus Himself said he did not come to destroy the law, but to fulfill it. The law of God is a friend to the righteous and comfort to the obedient. The law, if respected, is not hostile, but a thing to be feared by a reflection of the righteous character and intentions of God. It is God's will that we walk in wisdom and blessing.

The sins of the generations are ever present, influencing the shape and state of our lives long before we arrive on the scene. The devil knows more about our family histories and our ancestors than we do. He has been prowling through the corridors of our generations past as a lion, going about, seeking whom he may devour, as far back as Adam and the Garden. He is familiar with our patterns, pre-dispositions and most of all, our acts of disobedience, that have opened doorways into the living rooms of our lives. Those open doors have made it easy for him to access the soft, sweet, succulent flesh of God's flock down through the generations.

Our transgressions, the acts of crossing the boundaries of the law, have separated us from God. The law was set up like divine fence to keep the sheep in, and the lion out. Many of God's sheep, however, have chosen not to stay within the parameters of His protection and have wandered out into the killing fields of sin. Sheep are defenseless and vulnerable outside God's sacred and sure protection. When we disobey, we are on our own. God's protection has not moved, we have. Sin has taken us across the line into the devil's domain where Satan has convinced us that the grass is greener on the other side of the fence. God's blessing and protection are being traded for temporary comforts of fun and false freedom. Only later do we recognize the reality of our situation and our captivity to Satan is real.

WHY ISN'T THIS WORKING?

Like a fort with its gates left open, so a life traumatized and abused by the willful and ignorant acts of sin and neglect by the previous generation, is vulnerable and unprotected. Open doorways in our lives make the defense of the soul difficult, if not impossible. The sins of the generations become the entry points and main target areas for Satan's attack. Just as most of the traffic will come through the doors of the house, the enemy moves freely in places where our temple has been weakened by sin and our resolve has been overwhelmed by the attacker. He is familiar with the patterns of vulnerability created by the sinful choices of those who have gone before us and plans to take full advantage of them.

HUMAN PREDISPOSITION

Pre-dispositions are weak spots in the wall that, if pressed enough, may give way to become doorways or points of entry. Though these openings are in the past, they have provided the enemy with access into our life. Examples of medical pre-dispositions to alcoholism, diabetes, and high blood pressure alert us to the possibility of a higher percentage of incidences in those lives then are found in the general population. Generational sins operate in a similar way. The particular sins your generation practices have weakened your defenses against that thing. Because the enemy likes to win the game with the least amount of resistance, he will hit most of the balls to the weak spot in the playing field. This sets people up to experience a higher incidence of trouble in some areas than in others.

Predisposition to sin must not be confused with sin! Predispositions are not sins, but a measure of weakness. Predisposition is the tendency and probability of someone falling into sin. Part of those that often give way to sin expresses their "humanity", as "I'm only human.", or "It's human nature." The flesh is our propensity to sin and gives permission to our weakness. Our human nature sits, like the weakest links in the chain of grace, ready to burst the minute things get hard. If a chain is only as strong as its weakest link, the predisposition of these weak spots makes them the first places to break. The enemy is very familiar with our particular weaknesses. He has been observing our behavior ever since it was first formed and acted upon by our great, great, great grandfathers long before we even existed. As these behaviors are repeated from one generation to the next, they form consistent patterns that can be predicted.

WHERE TO START

When looking for patterns, it is always easiest to start with things you can see. Family histories can be fairly accurate tools in predicting problem areas and patterns. As we study them, we must try to stay objective and open. Identify the behaviors and bondages you observe among the members of your family. Don't forget to include things in your own life. Do not justify or minimize these things, but take a "fearless moral inventory" as those in many recovery programs are taught to do. Do not overlook family stories and legends or oral traditions like, "Your aunt Sally takes after the Andersons," or "No one knows much about Uncle Milton who seemed a little different..."etc. These kinds of statements often furnish valuable information that is easily overlooked as gossip or old wives tales. That they might be, but the fact that the information has hung around so long in the family indicates that people have noticed a pattern of reoccurring phenomenon and the information might be true.

Observing siblings, and asking the question, "How are they doing now?" often turns up valuable information about the family blood lines in terms of curses and blessings. Although we do not rely solely on opinions or family gossip, we do well to not discard it. It may reveal a spirit of strife and jealousy or deception present within the family. There are some excellent materials available to help you ask the questions and includes areas you might overlook. Sometimes the insight of a trusted friend, counselor or pastor can help.

Another question to ask concerns the general well being and ability of the family to flourish. Is there a history of long-standing sickness, early and untimely death through sickness or accidents, and chronic poverty? Do the members of the family have children out of wedlock? Is there a history of sexual abuse, mental weaknesses, violence, hatred, occultic activities, psychic powers, or curiosity for the things of the occult. Were members of the family into witchcraft, the Mafia or the Masons?

These are questions that can reveal the tangible ways in which the devil might be trying to collect on the unconfessed sins and open doorways he's found available in our lives. Careful observation reveals the methods and routes most frequently used by the enemy. In your reflection, what family traits stand out as most noteworthy? Are your family members known for their honesty and integrity, or for their general disregard for moral values and truths? Are they characterized by their tempers, addictions, jealous and competitive attitudes? Do they display lying, controlling and judgmental attitudes, or sexual perversions?

Does mental instability or divorce run in your family? How well are your siblings doing? Are they struggling emotionally, physically or financially? Is your experience similar to theirs? Do you see your children's lives beginning to repeat the patterns of abuse and failure you have worked hard to overcome? Are the members of your family open to the gospel and receptive to truth, or are they silent, secretive and cold?

Do you experience perpetual poverty? Does it seem that no matter how hard you work, finances are a continual concern? Is your family, or personal life plagued with sickness, or patterns of tragedy? God's instruction to His children as they came in to repossess the Promised Land was very clear. "Do not follow after their gods, inquire after them through the use of soothsayers, mediums or wizards. For all who do these things are an abomination to the Lord." Deuteronomy 18:9-12. Anyone who is an abomination to the Lord is not on His list of blessing. Answering these questions frankly and fearlessly will give you a place to start in tracking down the enemy and locating the open doors in your own life.

DEUTERONOMY 27, THE SINS

Deuteronomy Chapters 27 and 28 give a fairly extensive and interesting list of specific behaviors that bring a curse. A curse is not only the absence of a blessing, it is an antagonistic assault against a life for the purpose of destroying it. The list of curses begins in Deuteronomy 27:15 start with idolatry, worshipping something other than the creator. The second behavior that brings trouble is to the one who "treats his father or his mother with contempt", Deuteronomy 27:16. How many young people are suffering from despising their parents? The list of abominations in Deuteronomy 27:17 goes on. "Cursed is the one who moves his neighbor's landmark," robbing him of what is rightfully his. "Cursed is the one who makes the blind to wander off the road." Deuteronomy 27:18. Cursed is the one in who is deceiving the helpless, or takes advantage of his neighbor's misfortune. "Cursed is the one who prevents the justice due the stranger, the fatherless and widow," Deuteronomy 27:19, and the one who takes the needs and rights of others lightly.

In Deuteronomy 27:20, God addresses the sins of lust and incest. These are huge openings for evil. The Word covers this one from almost every angle imaginable. If we keep in mind the seriousness of sexual sins because of the shame and devastation they bring into the life of those involved, and the serious spiritual damage they bring, we will more well understand the wrath they draw from the Lord. Incest breaks the rules and violates the most sacred boundaries of human conduct, causing us to sin against our own selves. A life touched with incest and sexual abuse may be damaged and shattered on every level, mental, emotional and physical. Healing those breaks is something only the Master can do.

DEUTERONOMY 28 – THE PROMISES

Deuteronomy 28:1 brings hope and the promise. We are admonished to "diligently obey the voice of the Lord {our}your God, to observe carefully all His commandments." Pay strict attention, He says. Be careful! Don't read over this too fast. In Deuteronomy 28:20 God says "The Lord will send on you cursing, confusion and rebuke in all that you set your hand to do..." In verse 22 "The Lord says that He will "strike you with consumption, with fever, with inflammation, with severe burning, with the sword, with scorching and with mildew." God gets specific. Disobedience brings specific consequences that affect everything. Verse 27 warns that if we choose to deny God, the "Lord will strike you with the boils of Egypt, with tumors, with the scab, with the itch from which you can't be healed." Verse 28 brings the curse of mental instability and insanity. "The Lord will strike you with madness and blindness and confusion of heart."

The Lord continues the list of maladies. In verse 29 He prophesies that "you shall grope at noon day, as a blind man gropes in darkness; you shall not prosper in your ways; you shall be only oppressed and blundered continually and no one shall save you." Verse 35 says, "The Lord will strike you in the knees and on the legs with severe boils which cannot be healed, and from the sole of your foot to the top of your head."

The list is incredibly specific and sounds like a litany of complaints recited thousands of times every day in the doctor's office. It describes, all to well, the conditions and personal lives of too many of us. Why are all these bad things always happening to us? How long can those with allergies breath in pollen before it irritates their nasal passages? How much more careful are we to avoid the poison ivy then we are in avoiding the pitfalls of sin. We fail to heed the warning about those shiny leaves of sin, never suspecting the plague of itching and burning and blistering that comes from touching them. God does not afflict us needlessly. He does not want us to be overtaken, or destroyed because we are unaware of the consequences of actions that at the time had seemed so trivial and insignificant. God is not nit picking without a reason. We would be better off if we understood the reason for our troubles then to argue with or ignore them.

God doesn't want us to be ignorant of the present condition of the earth and the general prevailing curses that operate on it. Every thistle in our fields, and every painful contraction in delivery attest to the ongoing connections between modern civilization and its ancient roots in Eden.

God says be diligent. Be careful. God's Word is no respecter of the ignorant or innocent. Disobedience makes us vulnerable to the consequences of disobedience. Obedience breaks the curse and stays its effects. Some of us have been walking in a poison ivy patch of sin, ignorant of its connection with the blistering itch and watery eyes of our lives. Deuteronomy 28:45 & 46 go on to re-emphasize the word, just in case we missed it the first time, "Moreover, all these curses shall come upon you and pursue and overtake you, until you are destroyed, because you did not obey the voice of the Lord your God. And they shall be upon you for a sign and a wonder, and on your descendants forever."

LEVITICUS 26:39-40 - THE INIQUITIES

Leviticus 26:1 says "You shall not make idols for yourself; ..." "You shall keep My Sabbaths and reverence My sanctuary; I am the Lord." But is He? Do we think much of the Lord's commandments or take His Word that seriously in our life? Have we not reduced the Word of the Lord to a matter of options and opinion rather then obligation?

Leviticus 26:14 &15 goes on to contrast the blessings with the curses; "But if you do not obey Me, ..." and "if you despise My statutes, or if your soul abhors My judgments, so that you do not perform all My commandments, but break My covenant,"… " I also will do this to you: I will even appoint terror over you, wasting disease (AIDS, maybe?) and fever which shall consume the eyes and cause sorrow of heart.," Leviticus 26:16. He says that He will "set His face against us.", Leviticus 26:17.

Leviticus 26 goes on to describe curses that will reign over our planting and harvest, and set those who hate us to rule over us. Disobedience will cause us to flee when no one is chasing us, and bring us humiliation. The Heavens will be like iron and the earth like bronze. We

140

will labor in vain and our land and businesses will be unproductive. He will multiply our consequences seven fold and even the wild beasts will come in out of the fields to terrorize us, our children and our animals. The roads will be deserted and the sword will come against us. Pestilence will come into our cities and we will not have enough bread to eat. There will be shortages and we will go hungry. Horror of horrors will come to the point that we will even eat the flesh of our own children if we persist in our abominations and idolatries. The Lord says He will not put up with it any more, and even if He should delay because of His longsuffering, we can be assured that His wrath will come.

THE LAW

God does not want us in bondage to the law, but He cannot have us ignorant of it either. He takes a lot of time in Romans and Galatians to explain things about the law. Do Deuteronomy and Leviticus have a place in New Testament living? What happens to the conditions of cursing and blessing for the followers of Christ?

The law is still the law, "our tutor to bring us to Christ," Galatians 3:24. The law is now fulfilled in Jesus who reminds us that the Spirit of the Law has prevailed over the letter in that, the letter kills but the Spirit gives life, II Corinthians 3:6. All the law is fulfilled in this, that you love the Lord your God with all your heart, mind, soul and strength, and your neighbor as yourself, Galatians 5:14 and Matthew 22:36-40. The curse of the law looses its power in obedience. Nothing else has changed. Humankind has not suddenly gotten better, and the Lord has not lowered His standards or changed His mind about our need for a Savior. The law has not gone away, nor are Christians exempt from the root because they eat of the fruit.

The law stands as a book of firm declarations that have power to require certain things of us. The law respects and protects those who honor it. The patterns and promises first spoken in the Old Testament are as true today. The conditions for freedom are the same. Those who would trespass against it become debtors to it.

LEGALISM

God is drawing the line very straight and making the instructions very clear. He is not trying to strap us with the restrictions of religious ritual or legalism. He wants to help us find the way to walk in freedom. As the body serves as a container in which to hold the spirit, the law provides structure to freedom. Freedom is the end of the law to all who obey it. Observing the law enlightens us along the path to blessing. Observing the law is not a substitute for the cross, nor does it undo the work of the power of grace. The cross satisfies the legal charges against us by completing the legal obligations of the human race toward God, but do not be confused. Just because the sentence for the crime has been served, does not mean the prisoner, now released, can return to his or her lawlessness without consequence. We are still under obligation to obey the law of love, which was always the spirit of the law, even from the beginning. As long as we live we remain citizens of earth and stay under the jurisdiction of the laws of earth. Those laws must be obeyed to stay free.

IF...THEN

The Old Testament is as much His Word and as precious and powerful as the New. Leviticus 26:39-41 instructs us to repent for our own sins and confess the sins of our generations past. Why would God say that if it wasn't important? Throughout the whole chapter, God warns the Israelites about the consequences of disobedience and failure to come clean in their service to Him. "If you will, then I will" fills the chapter. "If you will not walk in My statutes...". What follows is a solid list of

My statutes...". What follows is a solid list of consequences that accompany disobedience. Deuteronomy 28:15 says "it shall come to pass, if you do not obey the voice of the Lord your God, to observe carefully all His commandments and His statutes which I command you today, that all these curses will come upon you and overtake you."

However, if we walk in His statutes and keep His commandments and perform them, then He will give us rain in its season, fruitful fields, abundant harvests, bread to the full and safety. He will give peace and victory over our enemies. He will multiply us and confirm His covenant with us. Moreover, He will "walk among you and be your God and you shall be My people," Leviticus 26:12. In Leviticus 26:13 God declares, "I am the Lord your God, who brought you out of the land of Egypt, that you should not be their <u>slaves</u>. I have broken the bands of your yoke and made you walk upright."

He sets us free and wants us to walk as free men. The law of God is not a restriction to the obedient man. He never even notices the walls of its perimeter that stand strong to insure his protection from the invader, because he never lives at the edge of his obedience, seeing how far away he can walk and still maintain the boundaries of God's blessings in his life.

PROVERBS 26:2 - THE CURSE WITHOUT A CAUSE

Proverbs 26:2 says that the curse without a cause does not come. That means that what things we see operating in the visible world have their origins in the unseen. Just as a great tree has a massive system of roots, so the great difficulties and often times recurrent family tragedies we see, do not spring up out of the air. There is an explanation. There is a reason. There is a cause for everything. Nothing just "happens".

If some things were the result of luck or fate, as

the universe, and He would not, by definition, even be God. God is sovereign and yet, in His absolute power, He limits himself to work within the context of the mind and will of human beings. However, just as He does not always and immediately interfere with the will of man, (and is often misunderstood and criticized for not doing it), He does not often intervene between the laws that govern sowing and reaping, or cause and consequences. He limits Himself to keep within the parameters of these laws, as surely as He abides by His "Universal Code of Justice," through which He governs the cosmic regions of eternity.

He has established these laws to make sure things operate properly, in balance and harmony. Through the law He maintains the integrity of the earth's environment, and insures justice for the weak and equality for the poor. The law never grows old or forgets. It sets the pace and keeps the peace from generation to generation. It provides the standard and the continuity for life to follow life.

CLINGING CURSES

Every curse has a source, a root, and a reason why it can operate. Curses come in many forms and can affect any area of a person's life. The curses cling to the fabric and fiber of a life until we become so accustomed to their presence and they become so familiar to us, that we do not oppose them or recognize them as the handiwork of the enemy. We are confused about many of life's tragedies and spend a lot of time asking, "Why?", never really expecting to get an answer. How many of life's tragedies could be avoided if the cause of the curse were identified in time to break it before it has stolen from us?

God desires that the enemy's cunning be exposed and the power of the curse be broken. Galatians 3:13 is a powerful verse, "Christ has redeemed us from the curse of the law, having become a curse for us, for it is written, "Cursed is everyone who hangs on a tree." Paul says the curses have been already paid for and were all absorbed in the body of Jesus as He hung dying on the cross. Jesus Christ served our sentence. His actions absolved us from the death sentence and its demand that one die. His death, however, does not give us a license to sin, though it provided us with a way to live. By his stripes we are healed. Scripture says Jesus took all our iniquities and became a curse for us that we could go free. He paid the price. The enemy continues to try to double bill us for crimes Jesus has already covered when He became a curse on the day His broken body was sacrificed.

The Bible declares that curses come through the practice of sin, idolatry and witchcraft, and can be more subtle then we first imagine. We may deny being idol worshippers because we do not bow to a golden calf in our back yard, or dress in black and participate in human sacrifices, but how much of the time are we only fooling ourselves, rewriting God's commandments to justify our lifestyles. Curses can be prayers and incantations spoken over people, places, or things which give the devil and his evil spirits operating privileges in their lives and those situations. Words spoken in anger or even with good intentions, that label and discourage or limit goodness and hope in our children's lives, can become curses in the hand of the enemy. Names we call our children in fits of rage or even in fun can become powerful life directives. "Slut, whore, liar, stupid, and you're just like your father or mother" are examples of words turned to curses we carelessly put on our children.

Curses pronounced over us by ignorant caregivers and those in authority over us become internalized. "Your are so stupid." becomes "I am so stupid." Saying "I am stupid" opens the door for the dull spirit who specializes in stupidity, to begin operating and interfering in our lives and learning processes. Who is to say that it does not open the doors for failure, dyslexia and attention deficit?

learning processes. Who is to say that it does not open the doors for failure, dyslexia and attention deficit?

Sometimes, however, the curse lies within our own mouth. Many times we bring curses upon ourselves by the things we speak over ourselves or one another. Jennifer was a Christian who had experienced severe emotional and sexual abuse growing up. Over and over, growing up she had cursed her life by wishing she were dead. She had began to experience strong physical attacks and sharp stabbing pains in her pelvic area, not uncommon experiences for victims of sexual abuse. She became more tormented and began to "see" the grim reaper that tormented her mind.

The Holy Spirit began to remind Jennifer of all the times she had wished she could just die. She had opened the door to an evil spirit who had come to oblige her. She had cursed her life with her own words in making the death wish. Her words had given the evil spirit legal right to come in and hurt her, because she had given it permission. She immediately repented and asked God to forgive her of her sin and resisted the spirit of death that had come in through the open door. The curse was broken and the apparitions of the death spirit left. The Lord is continuing to heal her through His Word.

Curses are the general outcome of a life of continued disobedience. Because they can be one of several maladies that plague our lives, it is not always easy to say in particular, which things have caused our condition. The physical, emotional, mental and spiritual difficulties we experience can be caused by a number of things. Many times it takes honesty and persistence to work through the labyrinth of contributing factors that manifest as an observable life problem. Curses are one of several general areas that need to be explored. If the "curse without a cause does not come", we know there must be a cause, a reason for the difficulty. If the Bible says that

"What gives the curse permission to operate in our life and who or what is behind it?"

If we can detect the cause, we are that much closer to solving the mystery of its insidious activity as it moves through our lives. If we can find a reason, we have hope to change the course of things. God has given us something we can do to remedy our situation, that we need not be caught in the circle of Satan's web, fated as victims of bad luck or bound in superstitions. Knowing there is a cause gives us hope that the cycle can be broken and we can be free to experience the new life of God's blessing. God wants us to be free to live apart from the curses of sin as they have operated specifically in our life.

OTHER OPENINGS

Many religious prayers and practices invite evil spirits to come and control people and manipulate situations. Native American medicine men, Eastern shamas, Hindu and Buddhist priests and monks, New Age spirit guides, witchdoctors and even born again believers are proficient in the art of cursing. How many Christians pray the problem instead of praising God in the midst of the problem? The more we rehearse the negative conditions, the more we give place to the devil to come and work in those conditions. Curses can be deliberate invocations spoken by one person against another, or they can be the result of personal sin. We must be careful that we do not serve the devil's purposed by the things we say and do.

IF WE WILL CONFESS THE SINS OF OUR GENERATIONS PAST

If we come from any ancestry where the one true God, the God of Israel, is not worshipped, and that is most of us, we would do well to confess the sinful misdeeds and practices of witchcraft, idolatry, and disobedience of our generations past, including their abominations and of us, we would do well to confess the sinful misdeeds and practices of witchcraft, idolatry, and disobedience of our generations past, including their abominations and atrocities and genocide against others. We confess their sins and repent of ours. Our confession takes away the devils claimed right to us. No longer can he hide in assumption and presumption. We have openly declared we do not want him, or acknowledge his plan as our own. Once this declaration is made, the demons usually leave. They can only continue to stay if a human part continues to give them permission to stay. This is where the love of Christ must persuade the human parts to believe in the goodness and sincerity of God.

Just a note of caution is in order here. Some childhood experiences are so shattering that there is more than one thing that must be done to restore the person. Many physical and spiritual and emotional conditions are not the result of one thing gone wrong. Often the enemy has networked and layered evil in our lives, that healing requires deliverance and inner healing in a number of areas before victory comes. The Word of God has the answers and those who seek the Lord for the solutions will find them. There is a cause for every curse, a reason for every condition, and a rescue for every prisoner. There is not a situation that has no answers as long as Jesus is truth and truth restores the soul.

SPECIFIC IS DYNAMIC

Every crime is committed in a moment in time. A deliberate act is done in a specific circumstance that allowed us to be victimized. To convict the criminal, we must prove him or her guilty of doing the thing they are accused of doing. To do that, we must present evidence that rules out their innocence. Unfortunately, most of us are very poor witnesses in our own lives, to the crimes that have been committed against us. We were attacked in a moment of vulnerability, like childhood and trauma, etc., and have no idea what happened. Some of us have been robbed blind and still have not noticed the jewels missing in the bottom drawer.

The more specifically the time and place and event are identified, the more confidently we can name the devil. The more specifically the work of the devil is named and the more completely the curses are identified, the more completely their power can be broken. The most effective way to deal with a curse is to identify how it operates in the life and when or where it got in. The practices of witchcraft, for example, which are huge open doorways for generational curses, are not always as obvious and easily detected as we might think. We have become so accustomed to some things they no longer appear dangerous. Reading our horoscopes, reading the fortune cookies, good luck charms, and participating in the rituals of various organizations are not the innocent and impotent sidelines we might suspect. Water witching, and superstitious religious practices that mingle with the Judeo-Christian truths, including praying to the dead, cannot be easily overlooked as harmless and innocent.

Witchcraft practiced at any level opens the door for trouble. Poverty, ongoing or frequent sickness, and premature death are all signs of the presence of witchcraft operating in our lives. If our family seems to be plagued with an unnatural number of disasters, or trouble seems to form a ring around us, we would do well to consider the possible presence of a curse.

CURSES ON OBJECTS

Curses can also come from objects and items over which invocation to evil spirits have been deliberately made. Voodoo dolls, New Age crystals and stones, demonic jewelry, trinkets, knickknacks, religious artifacts and souvenirs are some obvious articles that can carry becomes the unsuspecting recipient of the demon's activities in their life. Though they slip into our homes rather innocently, great damage can result, none the less.

Cursed objects are easy to deal with once they are found out. Unfortunately the delay can be very inconvenient and costly. The devil is no respecter of ignorance. Christians are as susceptible to the curses of objects as the unbeliever, though they are fully covered under their eternal life insurance. Just because we carry insurance does not mean we will not have an accident. The policy is there to protect from the consequences of the accident. So to, we are fully covered from loss through the Lord's provision, but we must submit a claim. If we allow the accursed object to continue in our presence, we will be under the influence of the demon behind that particular curse and without the Lord's protection.

Jan and Jeff had planned to spend a lovers holiday honeymooning in Jamaica. Their plans were abruptly changed when after only two days Jeff became desperately ill. They had stayed in an American hotel and had not eaten or drank outside the limits of safety as tourists are often advised. Even after their emergency flight to return home there was no improvement in Jeff's mysterious symptoms. Sharp pain pierced unpredictably through out his body, along with fatigue and cold sweats. After exhausting their medical options, finances became affected and the young couple became discouraged. Jan started to experience pain and infections of her own. Everything they had worked so hard for seemed to be vanishing into thin air.

Fortunately, they sought the Lord who led them to several passages in His Word, including Ezekiel 23:28-30 which talks about being delivered into the hands of those whom you hate who will take away "all you have worked for , and leave you naked and bare." It goes on to say, " I will do these things to you because you have ...become defiled by their idols. Deuteronomy 7:25-26 left no doubt in their minds. "You shall burn the carved images of their gods with fire; you shall not covet the silver or gold that is on them,…nor shall you bring an abomination into your house, lest you be doomed to destruction like it. You shall utterly detest it and utterly abhor it for it is an accursed thing." The Lord quickened to their remembrance a large wooden elephant they had purchased only several hours before Jeff had become so desperately ill in Jamaica six months before. Putting it all together, they remembered how dark and seductive the shop had been and how quickly they had wanted to leave after making their purchase. The end of the story proved the cursed object to be more then a theory. Jan was released from a bladder infection within the hour that the wooded idol had been chopped to pieces. On the same day that the elephant was burned, Jeff experienced marked physical improvement. The couple went on to experience full financial and physical recovery.

THE FORMULA FOR BLESSING

Because God does not always come down in crashing judgment against sin, we often miss the fact that God is quite specific about the results and effects of sin. We live feeling fairly secure, not thinking there might be consequences from our disobedience. This false security leads us to minimize or deny the presence of the curse because we have lost the connection between our sin and its consequences. If we would believe that through cause and effect, our choices create specific and predictable results, the outcome of our actions would never need be a surprise to us. The outcomes become as sure a certainty as any mathematical formula.

If we are open and believe what God says, it is easy to factor the equation for blessings and curses. If we know that X times Y equals Z and that one of the elements given in the equation is always the person involved in the that X times Y equals Z and that one of the elements given in the equation is always the person involved in the behavior, we can solve for the curse, (Y). The final outcome, (Z) is known, so all we need to find out is, what action, sin or behavior, when multiplied by the person, produces the behavior we see manifesting.

We see the results, mental instability, sickness, anxiety, confusion, etc. These are the outcomes the Bible describes as "not prosper[ing] in all our ways." Deuteronomy 28:28-29. What actions or sins proceed this oppression and cause the continual plundering? The "unknown" in this equation is the "Y" factor. Why me, God? Why did this happen to me? Why don't You do something to help me? The answer to this particular question is found in Deuteronomy Chapter 27, where God starts naming the bad things people do. Not only do they do them, in doing them there is a curse. "Cursed is the one who treats his father or mother with contempt." "Cursed is the one who cheats his neighbor, deceives the blind (take advantage of the vulnerable), perverts (twists) justice, or commits sins of incest, and sexual perversion in sleeping with relatives, one who attacks his neighbor secretly (is treacherous), or takes bribes to slay the innocent."

Me, (X), times my sinful actions, (Y) = curses, (Z). Using this mathematical principle it is easy to predict the results of ongoing and unconfessed sin in a person's life. Conversely, if I, (X) multiply myself by obedience, (Y), = blessings, (Z) will result in my life. It is the law of the harvest, sowing and reaping.

CONDITIONAL BLESSINGS, UNCONDITIONAL LOVE

Even though the blessings of God are conditional, His love is not! Love by definition cannot be conditional. He lets the rain fall on the just and the unjust. God's blessings, which are designed to lead us to spiritual maturity, however, are conditional and rest upon our obedience to His Word. Deuteronomy 7:12-13 says, "Then it shall come to pass, because you listen to these judgments, and keep and do them, that the Lord your God will keep with you the covenant and the mercy which He swore to your fathers. And He will love you and bless you and multiply you; …" It's not that He would not like to just out right bless us, but for now, He has an adversary who challenges His goodness to us as favoritism, and demands a full account be made for every blessing we receive. So God must continue to base His acts of goodness toward us upon our obedience.

CHAPTER EIGHT

THE POWER TO CHOOSE–DOES GOD DO IT ALL?

WHAT AM I SUPPOSED TO DO?

Many believers stumble in their walk with God. "Am I predestined or do I have a choice? What's God's part in all this?" It is the "If God wants me free, He knows my number," kind of thinking. We have a hard time finding the balance of power between free will and surrender in our walk with God. We stumble along the path of righteousness because we are confused about our role in partnering with God in the divine order of things. Our hesitation creates opportunities for the enemy to advance. Our uncertainty creates delays in accomplishing the work of the Kingdom, both in our lives and in the field. The issue must be settled before we find our proper place in God.

God is not a tyrant or a puppet master who pulls the strings to manipulate us into getting what he wants. Nor is He a magic stone that we can command to bring about a desired thing. Until we understand the true nature of our relationship with Him, we are prone to error. We will either become lazy and expect divine handouts or we will give up and drift in a fatalistic course without direction.

We must find the path between fatalism and rebellion. Just because God knows everything doesn't mean He asserts that knowing to accomplish everything that is known by Him. Nor does God get everything He wants, just because He's God and could have anything he wanted. The one thing He wants most of all only exists when it is freely given. That one thing is love. Love cannot be obtained through force or coercion. It only exists in the context of a will that is free not to give it.

So what is God's part in the redemption of His man/woman/child's fallen condition? Sin left us bankrupt, not only without good credit, but without a way to establish it. God, like a good father, who has the means to do it, put millions of dollars into our account. His death was the act of redemption that set up an unlimited bank account for us. Though He established and set up a personal account in my name, I will continue to live like a pauper if I so choose. Would it not behoove one so spiritually bankrupt as I, to get down to the bank, (the cross) and make a withdrawal?

No longer can we say that it is His "fault" if I go hungry or live without shelter. It is my move, but I must acknowledge my need before I will experience His abundance. We would do well to start to believe Him when He says there's money in our account, we would do better to make a withdrawal. We would do best if we would acknowledge His love and generosity with gratitude and stop grumbling.

The question is not what is God's part, but am I doing mine? God has done His part. God is not a complacent, non-caring or crabby deity that toys with His subjects. He continues to actively participate in our salvation. He left us clear instructions on how to do our part. His Word is full of instruction. It is the Word of truth that will set us free. He waits for us to step up to faith and actively enforce the victory of the cross and claim our promised inheritance in Christ.

Because God desires a relationship with us, He has limited Himself to allow us to participate in the management of His creation. He gave Adam and Eve the authority to run the Garden. They were given the right to choose and make decisions. God hoped, as any good parent would, that they would include His will in their decisions. He gave them the authority to accomplish the tasks of rulership and Satan was envious. That exercise of power, however, opened up the doors to endless possibilities for evil. Satan, motivated by his jealous, hateful nature, snatched their keys to the earth kingdom and stripped the couple of their dignity.

Since that time our battle to regain freedom has suffered at the hand of the devil's lies. He distorts the truth, knowing truth is the path to freedom. That path has been filled with dangers of every kind. Though confusion, doubt, false doctrine, and the constant assault of lies have left us defenseless and naked in the midst of the battlefield, Satan was never able to take away our freedom to choose. The Lord is sounding the trumpet blast, calling us to rally around our captain. He will strengthen our weakness and cause that which remains to be healed. Our strength will come in exercising the power to choose to do His will. In choosing to follow Him we declare war on the devil.

DESTINED TO WIN

For many believers, one of the most frustrating things about God is the mystery that seems to envelop Him. From our limited vantage point, He appears to be arbitrary and unpredictable. We suspect Him of favoritism. We feel predestined and fatalistic and discouraged. Prayers are prayed to no apparent avail. Nagging sins and habits persist. Answers don't come. We find ourselves asking, "What is wrong with this picture?"

The Bible says in Romans 8:28 & 30 that not only do all things work together for "good to those who are called according to His purpose," but that He called everybody. How do we know that? Lots of ways. Look at the group he picked the "called" from, ... those he "foreknew". Did not God "foreknow" every human, born or unborn that would ever be conceived? Everybody was foreknown. In our mother's womb, while we were yet unformed, He knew us. Those He "foreknew," He "predestined" to be conformed to the image of His Son. Again, that still includes the "everybody" He foreknew. So He predestined, declared beforehand, everybody He knew, which was still, "everybody." We can conclude that He "predestined" everyone to be conformed to the image of His Son and be saved! But here is where the sorting starts.

God is still inviting, "calling" everybody to the wedding, the marriage of the Lamb and His bride, but, do you accept every wedding invitation you receive? Maybe, for some reason, you are busy that day, or don't feel you want to be with those people or, have any one of a number of excuses not to go. You have the prerogative of choosing not to accept the invitation. Just as everyone who is invited does not attend, so, not everyone who is called responds to the call. Not everyone is going to be in heaven, but surely not because they were not invited. Some people choose not to. They refuse the invitation or don't realize its come. Failure to act upon the invitation is automatically declining.

God calls everyone, but is only able to justify those who respond to the call. Those who respond are redeemed. The blood is applied to their debt and their account is paid in full. They are candidates to being glorified. Only those justified are eligible for glorification. So who is against us? Is it God, or is it we ourselves, who have separated ourselves out from the grace of God's justification and mercy by our own reckless choices or careless oversight to believe the lies of the enemy?

It is our iniquities, our dishonest dealings that have separated us from God. Our sins and offenses against God have "hidden His face from us," Isaiah 5:9:2. Satan takes unfair advantage of us and our ignorance. It is to his advantage if we are sleeping, stupid (ignorant of God's promises and the power of those promises) or content to stay stuck. Only the blood of the Holy Lamb of God cleanses the unholy and makes the ground of our repentance the rock of strength.

come alive in Christ. If Satan can still control them through the cords of iniquity and the sins of the generations past and their own carnal and fleshly appetites, or the sinful wounding of others, he will do it. The Bible says that whosoever sins shall die. God declares "the life of the flesh is in the blood." Leviticus 17:11. The blood is equated with life and its absence is death. Leviticus 17:11 goes on to say He has given the "blood that makes atonement for the soul". When Christ shed His blood, He paid the price for sin by literally giving His Blood. Redemption was His life measured out in pints of blood.

The Old Testament covenant held in place by the blood of sacrificed lambs was no longer necessary. Through Jesus' Blood, final and full atonement was made for our souls. The rift between God and us was repaired in His separation from His Son. That separation was death. As the drops of His Blood trickled down, His life was poured out that we might live. It doesn't matter how oppressed or disease infested the life, the blood of Jesus was enough to bring that life back to God. He paid the debt, the wages of sin, to the last penny.

The blood cleanses the ground and makes it Holy. Any place in our lives that has been brought under submission to the Blood of the Lamb is no longer under the hold of Satan. Application of the Blood brings sanctification to that area of the life. The devil cannot stand on holy ground, nor can he stand against its power to protect us. Because Satan is not able to divest us of our wills, we are free to apply His death as payment for our sins if we so choose. Praying and asking God's forgiveness for the sins we and others in our generational line have done to violate His holiness, is the first step to breaking the devil's stranglehold on us.

done to violate His holiness, is the first step to breaking the devil's stranglehold on us.

JESUS BOUGHT OUR TICKET

Just as one man's sin brought us all under the sentence of death, one man's death set all men free. The death of Jesus was complete payment for every sin ever committed or contemplated. The price has been paid. The tickets to board the jumbo jet heading to heaven have been purchased. Our benefactor, Jesus Christ, has paid the full price. Each of us has a ticket with our name on it. The attendant is waiting to reserve our seat. All that remains is for us to decide to come to the ticket counter, identify ourselves, pick up our ticket and board the plane. There is nothing really predetermined and fatalistic about it.

FOR SUCH A TIME AS THIS

The church in days past has not educated us very well in this area of authority and "spiritual warfare". Now it is the craze. God is faithful to bring His revelation of truth to lives who have the mind to move with the Holy Spirit. He is the teacher, the source of enlightenment who reveals His truth at just the right time. "Blessed are the eyes which see the things you see; for I tell you that many prophets and kings have desired to see what you see, and have not seen it, and to hear what you hear, and have not heard it.", Luke 10:23-24.

The revelation of God's truth is like a room filled with objects and furnishings. Until the light comes into that room, the objects though present, are not distinguishable or even apparent. In the fullness of time, the Lord was revealed in the incarnation. The truths He reveals here are for such a time as this, end days weaponry to set the body of Christ free.

Our weakness sometimes comes in the form of ignorance. We do not know about, or understand, our authority as members of Christ's body. Does not the body have the same power and privilege as it's head? Is Christ not the rightful head, both of the body called His church, and of each individual member of that Church? If my head goes to visit a friend, my body must go also. If Christ Jesus has all power and authority as the legal heir of the Kingdom of His Father, then, as members of His Body, are we not joint heirs with him? In a very true sense, when we act in accordance with His will, His power becomes ours. He shares His place of rulership with us.

He has given us all power and authority. That authority is a legal extension of the very power He has. That same power that called Lazarus from the grave is available to and resident in every true believer who is acting in obedience to His headship, because every believer has the Holy Spirit present inside of him.

The Lord desires that we rise up in His name and go down and take back those things the enemy has stolen from us. Jesus told us how the enemy has only come to steal, kill and destroy. Jesus has come to help us get back what was rightfully ours. He came to preach the gospel to the poor and heal the brokenhearted. So many are in poverty, not just in the visible, natural sense, but in their souls. They're broken and ready to give up. Actually depression and the "I don't care." attitude are two frequent characteristics of those defeated by Satan. They have given up on themselves. They've relinquished ground to Satan's lies without much of a fight. He's more than happy to take advantage of any weakness in us and set up his stronghold.

SALVATION IN A LAND OF GIANTS

The devil doesn't have any qualms about maintaining his strongholds of fear and addiction in our lives. It's his hope that through these, he will again be able to establish his kingdom and enlarge his borders. He is undaunted by our verbal acceptance of Jesus Christ and our

Savior and Lord. The devil knows that just because a man is saved doesn't mean he is automatically sanctified. He persistently works his options to delay and destroy our hope in God. Salvation and sanctification are not the same process, although they are intimately connected.

Terri was experiencing suicidal ideation and was desperate. She was literally clinging to life kneeling crumpled at the altar. She was tormented by the accuser and believed she was beyond redemption although she had sincerely asked Jesus to be her Savior. Fear and unbelief gripped her heart. She did not understand how the Father could be so cruel to kill His own Son. "I thought God was mean to hurt Jesus like that", confessed the frightened human part. And how could He ever love and forgive her if He was that insensitive and cruel. It was marvelous to see how the Lord resolved this dilemma for her. He took her to the Garden of Gethsemane and let her see an angel ministering strength to Jesus. She saw Jesus being held in the Father's arms and realized He had not left His Son alone. She saw Jesus, unafraid on the cross, looking down at all the people with compassion and understanding and forgiveness. "He tricked me," she concluded, referring to the devil.

The enemy had tried to destroy her hope with his lie about the goodness of God, which would have worked, but for the faithfulness of God who brought her to the truth. Christians can continue to be oppressed by the devil, no matter how powerful and sincere their salvation experience. The devil doesn't just say, "Oh, excuse me, I see you're saved now, so I guess I'll be leaving." He is more committed to holding on then ever. The war has begun. Before that he may have left us lay, like a sleeping dog, undisturbed. But now he will fight us, with all he's got, because we have become his enemy. He may cause us to doubt our salvation or confuse us on what the salvation means.

WHAT ABOUT REPENTANCE?

It takes desperation to cut to the chase on this. It is time to change. But I've got to want it. There can be no more rationalize, blaming, or excuses. "But I have repented, when I got saved, and all those times the preacher calls us to the altar. Isn't that good enough? Sometimes the Holy Spirit's call to a deeper commitment is misread as "not being saved." It may be more about conversion and repentance, then salvation. If God sends Nathan the prophet comes to us, we need to admit, "I am the man," like David did.

To remain sensitive to the Holy Spirit is important to His work in us, but I may not always be the problem. Though repentance, as directed by the Holy Spirit is always good, but it may not be your personal sin that is creating the trouble in your life. It may be the sins of those connected with you through your bloodlines. Leviticus 26:39-40 talks about repenting for the sins of the generations past.

Arguing with why my lineage should be an exception to the depraved condition of the human race is pointless. We are in the New Testament where "old things pass away and behold all things become new." Yes they do! But how? Through the process of sanctification and reclaiming the ground the enemy stole. God told Joshua that the Promised Land, as far as the eye could see, was his. Then God charged him to go in and possess it, see Joshua 1:1-9. Having the Promised Land given to you and possessing it are two different things. To possess it, the children of Israel had to go to war. They had to rout and resist the enemy. The parallel holds as true for the human soul overgrown with sin and neglected relationship with God. We go boldly to claim the new creature's promises of the believer. We remind Jesus about His promise of coming that we might have life and life more abundantly.

Getting saved is an act of submission. Submission is repentance. It is re-establishing Jesus Christ in His rightful place as Lord in our life. Submission re-establishes the kingdom as His and the legality of His presence and new ownership. The former owner, the devil, has just been bought out by the Lord of creation. Jesus then gives the believer His authority and the power to back it up. Together they evict the devil. Why should he be allowed to stay? His legal rights to the property have just become invalid. Jesus has the nail prints in His hands, to prove He is the new and rightful owner. He bought us with His own blood, and paid the debt of sin with the exact wages it demanded, "Death!". Submitting to God is coming into agreement with the Holy Spirit about the condition of things, and agreeing with Him on what needs to be done to correct the situation. If the devil got in through our obedience and submission to him, he will be evicted by the same rule, obedience and submission to God.

THE POWER OF OWNERSHIP – TAKING BACK THE GROUND

God encouraged Joshua to go in and possess what had rightfully been given to him and his people. God didn't just hand it to them. Through obstacles they had to overcome, He taught them lessons in faithfulness and self-control. God is good and always does what is best. He doesn't just automatically wave His holy arm across the top of our cluttered desk and brush into the garbage can the mess our life had become. He beckons us to look into His Word and be healed. The owner of 40 acres of private hunting land need not even be in residence on the property for it to still remain in his possession. The contract for deed is his ownership document. Even in his absence, if someone should come up and camp on that property and begin poaching the deer and fishing the brooks, the property and its features, its landscape and animals, are still his. The evidence of ownership represented by those papers, though in themselves, weak pieces of paper, contain notarized words that attest to his payment and subsequent ownership of that particular piece of land. Furthermore, those legal documents are very specific in describing exactly what price of real estate it is he does own. It is the NE 1/4 of the NW 1/4 of the SE section of such and such township.

The words on that paper and the testimony of his payment give the holder of the contract legal right to manage and own that property. He has the right to go down and demand that the trespassers leave. He has the privileged right to call the appropriate authorities to enforce that demand. For too long, we have given up the ground in our souls to the lies of Satan, only to find the devil has used the power of agreement to steal from us the talents and dreams God has given us. The devil has his eye on enlarging his borders, that he might someday live in the house on the hill. For those willing to engage in spiritual compromise or sleep the fatal sleep of apathy, destruction is only a matter of time. Those unwilling to acknowledge the seriousness of his intentions are sure to fall prey to any number of spiritual attacks, including physical and mental and spiritual oppression, illness and death. God never intended for us to live in defeat, but in the overcoming victory of the death and resurrection of His Son.

Our earthly experience and the principles of ownership are patterned after from those above. The words and the contract for deed give the holder of that legal document the authority if need be, to call upon and use the power's that govern his rightful operation of the land. In like fashion, the words and witness of the Bible form the testimony, both new and old, of the legal document that Christ holds. It attests to His rightful ownership of us. It gives evidence of the payment made. It attests to His Father's endorsement. "We are His workmanship."

Ephesians 2:10. We are God's property.

As members of Christ's body we have the same power and privilege Jesus does when we use our authority in Him. As His workmanship, we are eligible for His protection. Christ would bid all that are His, to go down into the swamps and strongholds of our lives, and take His authority to oust the impostors. Using the authority we have as believers and knowing the awesome power of the person who backs up that authority, gives us courage to go forth.

Removing the impostor and deliverance of the human soul are quite the same. We already have every legal right to do it, but taking up those rights and suing the devil is up to us. Jesus does not take away our free wills. We can live with the trespassers violating our property if we so choose. We can live in fear, being intimidated by the threats of the impostor, listening to his lies and false accusations, even in light of Jesus Christ's finished work on Calvary and the indwelling of His Holy Spirit in us. The enemy is committed to staying. If we resist the urging of the Holy Ghost to deal with the devil, we only give him the opportunity to enlarge his borders; but if we would realize the devil doesn't have a legal leg to stand on and call his bluff, we would experience freedom.

Obedience to the Word brings us to the truth and truth is the path to freedom. Too many times, we do not recognize the fear and confusion and doubt and pain and turmoil and misfortune as the activity of Satan. We know God is sovereign and over all, and though He may permit suffering and affliction for a season, as He did with Job, it is not without purpose and reason. See Deuteronomy 8: 1-16. God does not intend as a parent, any more then you or I do, for His children to suffer endlessly to the point of defeat and death. God allows Satan to afflict us only until His purposes are accomplished in us. If the enemy has some claimed right, even to the property of God, it comes in the fact that we, as occupants, are co-owners with God. He will not act independently on our behalf without our consent. Satan knows how fair and firm God is on upholding us in our freedom of choice, and presses the point for all it is worth. As long as the devil can keep the fear and pain alive in us, we will continue to be bound in needless suffering. If only we would believe the promises and go in, like Joshua under the direction of the Holy Spirit, and begin to reclaim all that which is rightfully ours.

But to the contrary, many believers end up believing, much like the ten spies, that the giants have it. Unbelief puts us in the position of doing the devil's work for him. We listen to his lies and push the buttons of fear and pain ourselves. Once the devil has trained us to keep playing the lies through the system, his job is done. We have absorbed the lies of failure and rejection and keep them alive through our words, until they become so much a part of us that we accept them as part of our own self concept. Once any lie has moved from the mind to become a solid part of the thinking it formalizes into becoming part of our identity. From that point, it becomes very difficult for us to discern the error of it or divorce ourselves from the power of it.

THE POWER OF A WORD

Gods' Word created and settled the universe. His Word will remain the supreme authority when heaven changes its coat and earth passes away. The vast expanses of darkness were driven back as the myriad forms of life came forth at His simple command. Words are powerful. Life and death are in the power of the tongue. God has given us His Word as a defense against Satan. The Word of God in our mouth becomes a deadly weapon against the lies of the devil. It doesn't matter how weak or eaten through with holes our life has become, the Word of God remains invincible and powerful enough to defend and restore us.

God's Word establishes the Universal Code of Justice. Truth and freedom are based on that Code of Justice. An eye for an eye demands restitution and balance. Jesus Christ paid restitution. The devil no longer has any right to demand believers to pay again. If we understand the Law of God, and legal parameters within which Satan is allowed to operate and the power of our authority over him, we are well on our way to spiritual victory in returning to God's original intentions of blessing us.

Our salvation is established in hope knowing that justice will prevail because the Word of God is based upon the character of God. He reaffirms the eternal stability of His Word making it inseparable with His own nature. All creation will come into alignment with His justice in that day when every knee will bow and every tongue will confess.

God does not speak idle words. There is a specific reason for every word He says. Even the order of the word is not arbitrary. All things God says are specific and powerful. Jesus knew the truth and confidently spoke the words of His Father to defeat His enemy in every situation. We have access to the same powerful words as He did. Our confidence in this battle comes through our relationship with the Father. Though Satan seems to rule in the hearts of men, he cannot win. He works in darkness. He uses words to create the lie as the illusion of light. He tells lies and does not care if his lies contradict each other. He is pragmatic. Whatever he needs he uses. Whatever works is justified.

The final power of the Word comes not only in its ability to set us free, but to keep us free. Now, you are clean through the washing of the water of the word. The Word of God has the power to cleanse us from the stain of sin. The shame and guilt of our past can be removed by the washing of water of the Word. It can bring the recovery of innocence and the restoration of our relationship to the Father.

LIBERATING POWER OF OBEDIENCE

The working of Christ's power and authority in and through us only comes with obedience to the truth. The law of conquest and the law of freedom both require that to be truly free, we must be surrendering to the truth as revealed to us in God's Word. Truth is the only legal liberator. Obedience to anything else brings bondage, be it ever so unobserved or innocent appearing, at first.

The key to victory is surrendering to the right power. Surrendering control to God is the act of obedience that brings freedom. We give up control to gain control when we surrender to God. God's Word is full of instruction that is profound in its simplicity and yet powerful in its application.

Stopping the sting of death from the fiery serpents came when the children of Israel looked upon the brazen serpent. Moses raised that serpent on a pole as a symbol of the One who would defeat the serpent's bite. Just as the act of obedience in looking at the pole was able to heal all those bitten by the poisonous fiery serpents, we too will be healed by looking upon the crucified Son of God. Jesus took our infirmities and oppression and became a curse for us that we might be loosed from the pain of our afflictions and the sting of death.

Just as God demonstrated to Moses that deliverance was as simple as looking upon the brazen serpent, there is nothing we can do to add to the work of the cross and its power to liberate us, except accept it. He wants us to know how simple, yet significant our obedience is to the work of setting us free. God must have our cooperation in order to work His power in our lives.

Control is control. Sin is sin. War is war. Strongholds do not automatically disappear. The devil doesn't just excuse himself and leave quietly after Jesus comes in. We must actively cooperate with His coming in. If we believe that things change automatically, without our involvement, we are not only naive, but become a prime target for the ongoing working of Satan in our lives.

Israel had a physical enemy. Ours is not flesh and blood, but the lies we believe, "the powers and principalities and spiritual wickedness in high places." Ephesians 6:12. Israel had to come to God for help as they were greatly outnumbered most of the time. The odds forced them to depend on God. When they were clean and obedient, it didn't matter what the numerical odds were. When they had sin in the camp, it didn't matter how small their opponent was. Israel was defeated at Ai, a town they greatly outnumbered. Thirty-six men died on that disobedient day. They all suffered because of one man's sin.

It is not that much different today. God says the sins of the fathers are visited onto the children to the third or fourth generation. That's true. That's the way it is. But, if God is the "same yesterday, today and forever", Hebrews 13:8, then Calvary must have been in the original plan. The cost of sin was paid for by the death of Jesus Christ. The process of a new life begins with relinquishing our control to the lordship and control of Jesus Christ. It is not God's will that we stay under the bondage or our grandfather's sins through the control of Satan.

That is why it is imperative because, as long as we control our own life, we are slaves to the one who controls us, his majesty, the devil. To begin to experience the freedom from oppression and bondage, we must begin with submitting to God. Submission re-establishes ownership of the temple. Submission is accomplished initially through salvation. The surrender of our wills, the acknowledgment of our need, and our sin is enough for God to come in and set up His beachhead of righteousness in us. From there He expands His domain and establishes His kingdom.

FREE TO CHOOSE

Satan's strongholds within us are built by the lies we have come believed. Each man's error might be unique to him, but it builds a prison, just the same. We are held captive in Satan's citadel where each lie has become a brick and each fear has become a chain. Then we get saved. The light of the glorious gospel comes into our darkness. Salvation means Jesus has unlocked the door of my prison. We can be free. But the condition to freedom is to believe, and act on that belief.

The truth is that our freedom to choose has never been taken from us, even in the darkest days of our imprisonment when we may not have known anything about freedom or Jesus. Jesus said, "I am the door," John 10:7. Freedom only comes through Him. He said, "I am the truth," John 14:6. Freedom only comes as truth is applied to the lies we've believed. The bricks of our confinement are destroyed one by one, as the truth of God's Word is revealed and applied to our condition. Every time we choose to replace a lie with His truth, another brick is removed. Obedience to his Word is faith. Our faith becomes a hammer in the hand of God that breaks the grip of the strongman and destroys the walls that have held us. No longer do we need to be confined by sin or defined by its shame.

DESPERATION IS A GOOD THING

Desperation is God's way of challenging us to get out of our comfort zones and stop making the perpetual adaptations we need to keep those zones undisturbed. God is "provoking us to love and good works". He has not called us to adapt to this evil world, or to avoid it. He's called us to bear witness to his power and presence to bring people out of its awful grip. But how can He do that if we will not respond to take a risk, or are already so strung out that we have lost control of our own lives?

When we become desperate, a strange thing begins to happen. We gain a new awareness of the tight fit of the box we've been living in. We realize that things can't stay the way they were and we become too uncomfortable to let them remain as they are. Personal honesty says things have got to change. Our fear is overcome by desperation as hope begins to search for help. Hope brings us to the light and the light manifests the hidden works of darkness. The light brings us to the truth and the truth sets us free.

Desperation brings us to hope because, at last, we are willing to do something. Desperation is defined as "a state of hopelessness leading to rashness." From the bands of hopelessness and the struggle to survive, comes the energy to burst the bonds that bind us. God allows a certain escalation of trouble in our lives to get our attention. The purpose is to clarify priorities and provoke us to action. We have sat too long like the four lepers in II Kings, feeling desperate without a plan. They were going to die if they didn't do something. If they stayed sitting outside the city, they would die of starvation. If they went inside, they would die in the siege. The enemy had food. They decided to get up and go see if the enemy would throw them a few scraps? They were already lepers. What did they have to lose?

ENOUGH IS ENOUGH

They had gotten past the waiting and were not willing to tolerate doing nothing any longer. We must get to the place where we say, "enough is enough". They abandoned fear for the possibility of hope. The worst possible thing they could do was just sit there. Their desperation propelled them into action even as the angels of God were preparing a banqueting table for them in the tents of their enemy. All they had to do was get up and go after it. Isn't it just like God to feed us out of the hand of our enemy? What better way to display His power and provision as God, then when He prepares a table before us in the presence of our enemies? Psalms 23:5.

Are you at the place of personal desperation? Are you ready to say, "enough is enough" and let go of what is not working in your life? If you are, look God's way. He is here to show you the way to true freedom. We begin when we get up, like the four lepers, and go down to the enemy's camp and see what great deliverance the Lord has worked for us.

STOP, YOU THIEF

The next step is to stand up and put a stop to his thievery. Jesus said "how can one enter a strong man's house and plunder his goods, unless he first binds the strong man? And then he will plunder his house." Matthew 12:29. He gives a pretty straight forward explanation. The devil binds us, plunders our goods and eventually sets up himself as the new "strongman". He burrows himself deep within the stronghold of lies and uses misfortune, trauma and tragedy to begin the cycle of destruction. As he moves through our life and down into our bloodline in a predictable pattern of carnage, he devours our hope, our youth and or progeny.

The enemy comes to steal, kill, rob and destroy. He heads straight for the "valuables". His goal is to destroy the gifts God has given us before they can be used to destroy him. If someone has a gift of mercy, he will lead him or her into exhaustion and caretaking. If someone has a gift of exhortation, he will try to shut that person down with feelings of inadequacy or deceive them into thinking they are responsible to save the world. One time, an attractive young career woman came in, struggling with an affair she was having with her boss. They both claimed to be Christians. She had the gift of mercy and felt sorry for him. As she tried to help him feel better, Satan twisted her gift into adultery. Surely this was not the Lord's original intentions for her ministry, nor was it hers. After she realized the lies she had believed and embraced God's truth, she was able to escape the snare of the enemy.

The real surprise is not what the devil does. He is only acting according to his nature. What is the tragedy is that we, the heirs of salvation, commissioned to enforce the victory of Calvary, followers of the One who rose from the dead, and destined to rule and reign with Him forever, are letting condemnation, confusion and fear assail our resolve. The false reasoning and lies of the devil disarm us. The more we believe what he says as true, the greater the arsenal we give him to attack us with. Eventually the enemy's plan and purpose becomes such "daily fare" in our life that we play the destructive tapes ourselves. He's trained us to do his dirty work for him. We curse ourselves in our ignorance and the words of our mouth become a creative force to destroy us.

I am not the enemy. Jesus is my friend. The devil needs to be denounced, dismissed and deposed in the life of anyone who will live godly in Christ Jesus. The logic behind this is not earthshaking. The Word of God is clear on this matter. We have no excuse but that we have believed lies and taken the devil's recommendations rather than God's. We need to start where John the Baptist began. We must repent of our lack of fervor and our contentment to stay bound and stuck. What many of us need is a good case of desperation. Desperation becomes a force that motivates us to take the next steps to freedom, as we prepare to plunder the strong man and expose his strategy as we take the devil to court.

POSTSCRIPT

As I close this first volume a few final thoughts come to mind. I invite you to examine these things for yourself to see whether they are true.

Jesus "appointed the twelve that they might be with Him and that He might send them out to preach and to have power to heal sickness and to cast out demons," Mark 3:14. Our call is a call to personal freedom and divine purpose. As long as we are bound and divided, the enemy knows we will not stand or go forward to enforce the victory of the cross. He knows that it is in his best interests to keep us imprisoned in the stronghold of the lie. The Lord is interested in us overcoming the obstacles in our lives that we might fulfill the great commission. But, before we can commit ourselves to the work of freeing others, we must be free ourselves. How are we going to go and make disciples of all nations when we can't even subdue the carnal appetites and mental confusion rising in our own city-soul kingdom? Establishing His truth in our lives becomes the Father's greatest concern and chief business in redemption.

Many of us who would call ourselves Christians are tormented with guilt, uncontrollable addictions, fantasies, pain and physical maladies that become the center of our life focus. Many of the things we end up focusing on are distracters and idols, strange idols, but idols, nevertheless. Pain, anger and safety become the objects of our attention. Even the eradication of sin from our lives can become a preoccupation and substitute for relationship with Jesus Christ.

God begins our journey to freedom by way of the cross. He intends to make an end of the mess by starting over, not because He is mad at us, but because He knows redemption must be thorough. The work He does is not cosmetic reconstruction or fresh paint on worn out rotten wood, but a complete metamorphosis. To do this He must have more then our sporadic attention. Redemption requires our full and continual consent. Obedience affirms that consent.

The power of agreement referees who will move in our life, God or Satan. Because the outcomes of our live are determined by our obedience, God sets us free by inviting us to become bond slaves to Him. Obedience to God is the visible demonstration of our love for Him. The irony is that He sets us free through submission, by that which appears to be freedom's opposite; even as He brings us to life through death; that which appears to be life's opposite. To surrender our will and freedom of choice is not a one time thing, but a lifestyle. To find freedom through surrender is foreign to the carnal man and unreasonable to natural reason. We define freedom as a license to do whatever we want, when we want. In God's economy of things, we can only be free when we finally lay down our privileges to do what we want, when we want, for how long we like at the expense of whoever need be, and surrender to Him the task of righteousness and the procurement of eternal life.

FREEDOM'S KEY - A SURRENDERED LIFE

But, does it really work to live life in a total and constant state of surrender to God? Consider how many people who, by their own definition of freedom, free to do what they want, when they want, are doing a very successful job of managing their lives? Trust in God is replaced by the most elementary lie, the assumption that I am in charge of my own life and know best how to live it. But, to avoid assumption I must ask myself, "Where did I learn life?" Who is strong or smart enough to know when to stop or how to change? Most of us are more like a four-year-old in a well-stocked candy shop than a Christian surrendered to the life of Christ in us. How much wisdom and self control and submission to the truth would that child need to keep themselves from a cavity or a tummy ache in such a sweet bed of temptation?

Our first step is to admit we do not know how to live this life, as much as we try or as much as we would like to insist to the contrary. If we are smart, we will submit to God even in the face of Satan's loud protests, knowing that God is the One who loves us and it is He who has the power to gives us true freedom. The purpose for our freedom then becomes the freedom of others. The purpose for our healing becomes the healing of others.

If the healing and freedom of others is an intricate part of the work of Christ in His church, then freedom from the curses and the generational cords of iniquity is an essential part of the believer's life. With the transfer of the blessings from one generation to the next, we break the negative dysfunctional patterns of sin not only for ourselves, but for our children.

Trusting God needs to be our response to truth. Distrust and doubt are the lies of deception that keep us bound. When we embrace the truth, faith in Jesus Christ becomes more then just words. Faith, to be faith, must be translated into actions through obedience. Believing the truth precedes our actions to obey. Our obedience is faith activated and becomes the sign of our love for Jesus. The active embracing of the truth then is the first step in obedience to the Lord's commands and is the demonstration of our love for Him.

TRANSLATING SPIRITUAL TRUTH INTO TEMPORAL REALITY

We can only fulfill our life's purpose when we are free. God has a dream He has put in the heart of each one of us. Even as the enemy has tried to destroy the dream and steal the gifts before we can unwrap them, those gifts and dreams are not just for us. God has given us gifts and abilities to evangelize the lost. The enemy has stolen our weapons and tried to shut down the work of God by intercepting the army of God along the way. When we are unaware of the war, or so preoccupied with ourselves that we fail to submit to the strength of our God, we fail to walk in His leading as He intervenes through us into the lostness of the others. Just as we cannot freely give that which is still bound in us, it is only as we give them away, that the gifts and callings of God in us become our own.

The freedom truth brings to the inward parts of the heart begins the transfer of spiritual reality into the natural world. Pain and defeat and personal dissatisfaction, anger and addictions must give way to the truth that whom the Son sets free is free indeed. That revelation becomes the motivation to bring the spiritual realities of redemption to those still bound in the enemy's kingdom.

THE NEW CREATURE AND THE OLD MAN

Why don't we get this? If it were a simple matter of learning and unlearning, don't you think we would have gotten it by now? I grant you that both unlearning the ways of sin and putting on the new man created after the righteousness of Christ, have their place in the life of the believer, but the world's philosophy for treating human behavior as, "I learned to be bad, therefore I can learn to be good.", promotes frustration and a "form of godliness." These measures are called coping and come with a great variety of religious recommendations and rigid prescriptions for holiness. They often serve only to heighten our frustration and increase our sense of failure.

To credit bad learning for the sum explanation of our sin behavior is to ignore or deny what the scripture says about the nature of the condition of the unregenerated man. Romans 6: 11 admonishes us to "reckon yourselves to be dead indeed to sin, but alive to God in Christ Jesus our

Lord." It goes on in the next verse to say, "Therefore do not let sin <u>reign in</u> your mortal body, that you should obey it in its lusts." Something "reigning in" me tells me there is a little bit more to this "dying process" than just relearning. To boast that I can learn to be or do good without considering the innate condition of my soul, no matter how splendid the nature of the environment around me, is the definition of boasting.

A TIME OF WAR

We deceive ourselves if we think holiness, restoring the temple to its proper function as the dwelling place of God, is a matter of self-improvement. Learning to be good, and doing better springs from ignorance and independence and ends in a doctrine of good works apart from the work of Christ. Learning the ways of the Spirit must come as an act of submission and obedience to the Holy Spirit. That submission leads to war. The Bible, the field manual for that war, declares in James 4:7, we are to "submit to God. <u>Resist</u> the devil and he will flee from you."

To "resist" suggests combat or action, and is a far cry from the idea of learning or reeducation. Change and freedom come when we learn it is best to surrender ourselves with our notions and opinions, to the truth of God. Victory and liberty come from learning the strategy of Satan against our souls. We must arise "for we do not wrestle against flesh and blood, but against principalities and powers, against the rulers of the darkness of this age, against spiritual hosts of wickedness in the heavenly places," Ephesians 6:12. In Matthew 12:29, Jesus calls these unseen principalities and spiritual hosts of wickedness the strongman.

If learned behavior is the solution for sin, why did Jesus talk about how the violent must take heaven by force, Matthew 11:12? What reason would there be for His warning about warfare and the presence of a strongman in our midst if there was no conflict? "Can one enter a strong man's house and plunder his goods, unless he first binds the strong man? And then he will plunder his house," Matthew 12:29. The strongman plundering the goods of one who is weaker sounds more like a matter of war then of education or learned behavior. This is war! And though there is a proper time for both, blessed is the one who knows what time it is.

The only way to deal with the strongman is to resist him with the authority we have been given in Christ. The more we understand spiritual truth and the enemy's strategy the more effective we will be in taking back the things he has stolen from us. The bottom line is being obedient to the things we have come to understand; becoming "doers of the Word and not hearers only, deceiving yourselves," James 1:22. From this passage we see delayed obedience and disobedience both open the door to further deception. Deception is the rope the devil uses to tie us up. The power to rule and reign with Christ begins with resisting the lies Satan has planted in our belief box.

THE BODY OF CHRIST

This is all about Jesus, but Jesus has a body. How are we to make sense of this? For so long we have kept the focus on us. Satan has tried to stop the work of God by his lies and his distractions. God wants us to experience His goodness down here, not to spoil us, but to spoil the powers of darkness. Jesus said He has "given us authority over all the power of the devil and nothing shall by any means hurt us," Luke 10:19. Is that just for some of the time, or whenever we need it? God is faithful and committed to drawing us out of bondage to prepare us to wed His Son. For too long the body of Christ has been divided and separated from itself. So what will you do? Some are content to exist and get by. They sit back and rest in their salvation, unaware or uninterested in the plight of others.

Others are trying individually to do for themselves what can only be done by the body together. Some of us have developed such a strong delusion of independence that we think we can breath with our eyes and walk with our ears to the exclusion those parts designed to do those things.

One of the best advertisements for the truth and effectiveness of the gospel is to live in joy. Joy is the hallmark of a free spirit. The joy of the Lord is our strength. That strength in preserved in the righteousness of the indwelling Christ that lives in us, the temple made without hands. We are God's residence now upon the earth. He dwells in His fullness in those who fully give themselves to Him. As He brings them together these become the church, the body of Christ. They become the message of God's salvation incarnate as an army, a people and a nation. Where He was One, we are many. But like the tea cup, the gathering of many broken pieces does not promote the function of a tea cup as it was intended, any more then the gathering of the Lord's broken body can function to heal a dying world.

MAINTAINING OUR FREEDOM

If elephants can only be eaten effectively, one bite at a time, it is also true that lives are only lived one moment at a time. Each moment presents us with an opportunity to say "Yes" or "No" to God's purpose and plan for us. If we yield to God's will, we will grow strong. If we yield to the devil, we will shrink. To obtain the utmost freedom and productivity the farmer must devise a plan. The fields are planted, and watched over because each day not only brings opportunities for growth but threats to that life.

It is for freedom that Christ has come to set us free, Galatians 5:1, for "whom the Son sets free is "free indeed." John 8:36. And even as He has come to set us free, His Word will keep us free. The principles are described and outlined in this book. They have been applied to hundreds of people who have found victory and relief through these truths, but like any good thing, they need to be maintained. A strong hunger for the Word will ensure a strong warrior. A teachable attitude will create a humble disciple. We must stay in the place of obedience to the Truth, determined to walk in that revelation.

Maintenance is a personal responsibility. Prayer and personal devotion to the Lord are primary sources of life and strength. Taking quiet time with Him protects us and guided us into more and more of His abundant life. To kick back and think things will automatically fall into place, is a plan destined to fail. Follow up and lifestyle are an important part of recovery from surgery. We need to allow the Holy Spirit to adapt our lifestyle to that of living for Christ.

A second part of that personal responsibility is to finish the race. That includes accountability to the body of Christ and specifically to that place to which the Lord has called us. We put on the mind of Christ and no longer look to, or make provision for the flesh, to fulfill it's lusts. If we do these things Christ will be able to complete the good work He has begun in us, and we will be able to say with Paul in II Timothy 4:7 & 8, "I have fought the good fight, I have finished the race, I have kept the faith. Finally, there is laid up for me the crown of righteousness, which the Lord, the righteous Judge, will give to me on that Day, and not to me only but also to all who have loved His appearing." How can we improve on that? Only to hear Him say, "Well done, good and faithful servant. Enter into the joy of your Lord." Matthew 25:21.

EPILOGUE

"Present Your Case," is the first in a series called, "Taking the Devil to Court." It surveys the background and scriptural principles used to take legal action against the enemy of our souls. A crime has been committed! The villain has presented himself as an Angel of Light. He has lied to his victims and stolen their property and defrauded them of their inheritance. Understanding our authority as believers and the legal parameters of our life in Christ are essential to defending ourselves as we build our case in "Taking the Devil to Court."

To convict a criminal we must establish evidence and find a faithful witness. "Present Your Case," establishes the identity of the suspect and the fact that a crime has been committed. It reviews the evidence of a higher calling in a more abundant life and found it missing in many believers' lives.

"Opening Arguments" is the second book in the series. It will reconstruct the opening scenes that set up the plot. Understanding the origin of the conflict between God and the Devil enables the believer to build an airtight case against the enemy's accusations. It examines the motives and weighs the claims of Justice and Mercy as required by the Universal Code of Justice.

"Nothing But the Truth, So Help You, God," the third book, outlines the procedures for uncovering the lies that have become embedded in our individual lives and demonstrates the power of the truth to set innocent captives free. It reconstructs the scene of the crime and establishes the time it was committed. It uncovers in more dctail the methods the enemy used to accomplish his evil deeds and the procedures to undo it.

Every crime reveals a criminal and demands justice be served. To convict the devil of his heinous crimes against us we need evidence and a faithful witness. Every crime was committed at a place in time. To establish the guilt of the accused we must convince, beyond any shadow of doubt, the time, place, method and identity of the criminal; who, what, when, where, why, and how.

The Word of God declares justice is defined as an "eye for an eye," Exodus 21:24, blood for blood, life for life. Jesus paid the maximum penalty, death by execution, that we could go free. If He so freely spent himself for our liberty, would it not be His will that we walk that freedom? Whom the Son sets free is free indeed.

Ministry Page

LIFE RECOVERY

Life Recovery translates the scriptural principles described in the book into practical application and counseling techniques.

In addition to the book, we have developed a 72 minute 3 part video series that demonstrates some of the amazing new breathroughs in counseling that are revolutionizing peoples lives. "Taking the Devil to Court" is based on scriptural principles and Jesus Christ as the Wonderful Counselor. It diagrams the enemy's strategy against believers that often debilitates and devitalizes them to a point where they are stuck and unfruitful to the Kingdom of God.

Life Recovery is an independent Christian counseling service that is not affiliated with any other counseling agencies.

For more information on the counseling services, materials and workshops contact us at:

Life Recovery, Inc.

7671 Old Central Ave. N. E.
Fridley, MN 55432

(763) 785-4234
Fax (763) 785-4622

www.liferecovery.com

Other books you will enjoy reading

THE GOD CHASERS (Best-selling **Destiny Image** book)
by Tommy Tenney.
There are those so hungry, so desperate for His Presence, that they become consumed with finding Him. Their longing for Him moves them
to do what they would otherwise never do: Chase God. But what does
it really mean to chase God? Can He be "caught"? Is there an end to the
thirsting of man's soul for Him? Meet Tommy Tenney—God chaser.
Join him in his search for God. Follow him as he ignores the maze of
religious tradition and finds himself, not chasing God, but to his utter
amazement, caught by the One he had chased.
ISBN 0-7684-2016-4

GOD CHASERS DAILY MEDITATION & PERSONAL JOURNAL
by Tommy Tenney.
ISBN 0-7684-2040-7

POWER, HOLINESS, AND EVANGELISM
Contributing Authors: *Gordon Fee, Steve Beard, Dr. Michael Brown,
Pablo Bottari, Pablo Deiros, Chris Heuertz, Scott McDermott, Carlos
Mraida, Mark Nysewander, Stephen Seamands, Harvey Brown Jr.*
Compiled by *Randy Clark. Randy is also the author of "God Can Use
Little Ole Me."*
Many churches today stress holiness but lack power, while others dis-
play great power but are deficient in personal holiness and Christian
character. If we really want to win our world for Christ, we must bring
both holiness and power back into our lives. A church on fire will draw
countless thousands to her light.
"Caution: The fire in this book may leap off the pages on to the reader.
God's fire empowers, purifies, and emboldens our witness. This is the
way the Church is supposed to be. Highly recommended."
—Dr. Bill Bright, Founder and President
Campus Crusade for Christ International
"The future of the Church is at stake and this book has some answers."
—Tommy Tenney, Author of *The God Chasers*
ISBN 1-56043-345-0

Other books you will enjoy reading

NO MORE SOUR GRAPES
by Don Nori.
Who among us wants our children to be free from the struggles we have had to bear? Who among us wants the lives of our children to be full of victory and love for their Lord? Who among us wants the hard-earned lessons from our lives given freely to our children? All these are not only possible, they are also God's will. You can be one of those who share the excitement and joy of seeing your children step into the destiny God has for them. If you answered "yes" to these questions, the pages of this book are full of hope and help for you and others just like you.
ISBN 0-7684-2037-7

WHATEVER HAPPENED TO THE POWER OF GOD
by Dr. Michael L. Brown.
Why are the seriously ill seldom healed? Why do people fall in the Spirit yet remain unchanged? Why can believers speak in tongues and wage spiritual warfare without impacting society? This book confronts you with its life-changing answers.
ISBN 1-56043-042-7

To order these books, to order *Taking the Devil to Court,* or to contact Marjorie Cole, write or call:

Life Recovery, Inc.
8809 Central Ave. NE
Minneapolis, MN 55434
612-780-3531
1-800-270-9588-88
E-mail: drousu@uswest.net
www.liferecovery.com

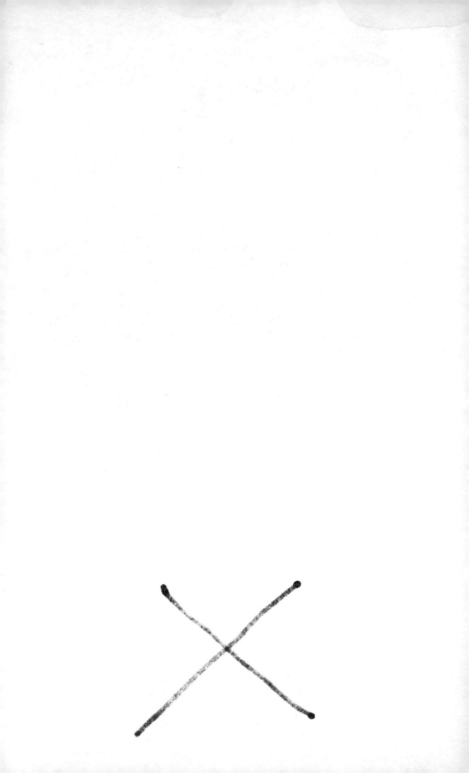